The Didsbury Lectures, 1985

THE RELEVANCE OF JOHN'S APOCALYPSE

The Didsbury Lectures

The Didsbury Lectures are delivered annually at the British Isles Nazarene College, Manchester. Previous series are available as follows:

BRUCE, F. F.   *Men and Movements in the Primitive Church*

MARSHALL, I. H. *Last Supper and Lord's Supper*

TORRANCE, T.   *The Mediation of Christ*

ATKINSON, J.   *Martin Luther: Prophet to the Church Catholic*

BARRETT, C. K.   *Church, Ministry & Sacraments in the New Testament*

THE RELEVANCE OF JOHN'S APOCALYPSE

Donald Guthrie

WILLIAM B. EERDMANS PUBLISHING COMPANY

THE PATERNOSTER PRESS

AUSTRALIA:
*Bookhouse Australia Ltd.,
P.O. Box 115, Flemington Markets, NSW 2129*

SOUTH AFRICA:
*Oxford University Press,
P.O. Box 1141, Cape Town*

British Library Cataloguing in Publication Data

Guthrie, Donald
    The Relevance of John's Apocalypse
    1. Bible. N.T. Revelation ——— Commentaries
    I. Title
    228'.06   BS 2825.3

    ISBN 0–85364–460–0

Library of Congress Cataloguing-in-Publication Data

Guthrie, Donald, 1916–
    The relevance of John's Apocalypse.
    1. Bible. N.T. Revelation———Criticism,
    interpretation, etc.
    I. Title.
    BS2825.2.G87   1987   228'.06   87–13677

    ISBN 0–8028–0329–6

Photoset in Great Britain by
Photoprint, Torquay, Devon,
and printed for The Paternoster Press,
Paternoster House, 3 Mount Radford Crescent, Exeter, Devon,
and William B. Eerdmans Publishing Company,
255 Jefferson Ave., S.E., Grand Rapids, Mich. 49503, U.S.A.
by A. Wheaton & Co. Ltd., Exeter, U.K.

Contents

Preface

The four chapters of this book formed the subjects of the four Didsbury Lectures for 1985 delivered at the British Isles Nazarene College, Didsbury, Manchester. The intention behind this series of lectures was to bring out ways in which the book of Revelation might have practical applications for the church of today. It is because of this essentially practical purpose that the overall message has been emphasized rather than detailed points of exegesis. Too often the main thrust of the book has been submerged in a plethora of opinions regarding the significance of the book for the future. It is hoped that the publication of these lectures will lead many to a greater interest in a part of Scripture which is often regarded as a closed book.

I would like to express to the faculty of the Nazarene College my warm appreciation of their fellowship during the days I spent with them. I would also like to thank the audiences at each of the four occasions for giving me such a sympathetic hearing.

Abbreviations

ATR	Anglican Theological Review
BA	Biblical Archeologist
BJRL	Bulletin of the John Rylands University Library of Manchester
CBQ	Catholic Biblical Quarterly
EQ	Evangelical Quarterly
ET	Expository Times
EvT	Evangelische Theologie
JBL	Journal of Biblical Literature
JTS	Journal of Theological Studies
NTS	New Testament Studies
NovT	Novum Testamentum
PG	(Migne) Patrologia Graeca
PL	(Migne) Patrologia Latina
RB	Revue Biblique
TDNT	Theological Dictionary of the New Testament (ed. G. Kittel. Eng. tr. G. W. Bromiley)
ThZ	Theologische Zeitschrift
TLZ	Theologische Literaturzeitung

The Content and the Search for Meaning

CHAPTER ONE

The Content and the Search for Meaning

Anyone approaching the book of Revelation is likely to be aware of the difficulties of this book. Most people indeed adopt the view that it is too difficult to have much relevance for our modern times. It is couched in such obscure language that the modern reader at once turns away from it, although not without some perplexity since it is part of the canon. It is so full of strange visions, fantastic imagery, amazing events, intriguing numbers, without any clear clues about their meaning, that anyone can be excused for thinking the safest thing to do is to leave it alone. Such an approach has had some famous representatives. Luther regarded the book as a dumb prophecy, while Calvin never commented on it, and Zwingli could make no sense of it.[1] At the other extreme, many have majored on the book as the key for the understanding of the whole New Testament.

---

1. Luther relegated this book, together with James, Jude and Hebrews, to the end of his New Testament. He did not consider it to be an inspired book. Zwingli also did not regard it as a biblical book.

Between these two extremes are a host of more cautious approaches, which admit it has some relevance, but which avoid being dogmatic. Indeed, if the history of interpretation of this book can teach us anything it must be to warn against an over-dogmatic attitude of mind. It is a bold person who dares to say that he has cracked the code of the Apocalypse. But those who avoid the book because of its difficulties are in danger of losing the exhilarating experience of searching for its modern relevance.

A Brief History of the Search for Meaning

In the early church this book was variously received, but by the time of Justin we know there was widespread interest in it. Justin adopted a chiliastic view, considering that it taught a literal millenial kingdom,[2] and in this he seems to be reflecting a currently held view. A similar view was advocated a little later by Irenaeus.[3] For him the Roman Empire represented the anti-God power, although he did not identify it with antichrist. Although adopting a mainly literal view, Irenaeus mixed this with some symbolical interpretations. Another chiliast was Hippolytus[4] who thought that the millenium would start in AD 500, but regarded it as an earthly rule of Christ. He relied much on the book of Daniel as his key for understanding this book and identified Babylon with Rome. Hippolytus wrote during the period of opposition between the Roman empire and the

2. *Dial. c. Trypho,* 81. He found support for his chiliastic views in Rev. 20.
3. *Adv. Haer.* V. 3, 30
4. In his tract *On Christ and Antichrist,* 24ff in Lagarde's edition.

church. He was therefore convinced of the present relevance of this book. It was Victorinus[5] who was the first to appeal to the Nero redivivus myth for an understanding of the Beast, and he was also the first to use the recapitulation theory for an understanding of the different series within the book of Revelation.[6]

A different approach was developed by Origen,[7] who was opposed to the literalism which was so characteristic of Jewish apocalyptic. For him the key to this book was to treat it as conveying spiritual truths. Antichrist becomes not so much a person as a system of evil. Just as in his general approach to the interpretation of Scripture Origen considered the allegorical meaning to be more important than the literal, so in his understanding of this book he regarded the spiritual meaning as superior to any other. A similar approach is found in Methodius,[8] who interprets the visions allegorically. Both Origen and Methodius, for instance, treated the heads of the dragon as seven sins.

One writer who exerted great influence on those who came after him was the Donatist Tyconius,[9]

---

5. *Commentary*. The extract published by Haussleiter, *Theologisches Literaturblatt* 26 (1905) col. 192ff. Victorinus wrote the earliest extant commentary on the book. Although advocating a recapitulation theory, he nevertheless acknowledged a chronological element.

6. J. M. Court, *Myth and History in the Book of Revelation,* London 1979, 5, suggests that Irenaeus was the real source of the recapitulation theory. For an explanation of the recapitulation theory, see below, pp.00.

7. *De Princ*, ii.11.13. Cf. C. K. Barrett, *Cambridge History of the Bible* (ed. P. R. Ackroyd and C. F. Evans) vol 1, Cambridge 1970, 379, who points out that Origen's method maintains the authority of the book but destroys its historical meaning.

8. *Symp*. viii. 4ff.

9. For details cf. H. B. Swete, *The Apocalypse of St. John,* London, 1906, cxcvii.

who regarded the Beast as representing the
Catholic hierarchy and the Donatists as the true
church. His treatment completely ignored the
historical circumstances of the original readers,
and concentrated on the spiritual meaning. He
had no doubt that the book was highly relevant for
his own age. An example of his interpretation is
his view that the two witnesses are the church
preaching Christ in the two testaments. There is
no need to identify the Beast because he represents
world power. Indeed, for Tyconius recapitulation
was of a spiritual kind which emphasizes the
totality of the spiritual forces. A similar kind of
interpretation was followed by Augustine,[10]
although from an orthodox point of view.

From Augustine to the fifteenth century the
spiritualizing method was dominant, although
there were a few who followed the more literal
interpretation. Men like Andreas[11] of Caesarea
and Primasius[12] of Hadrumetum both pursue a
spiritualizing line similar to that of Tyconius,
although without his Donatist emphases. These
men shared the view that the millenium which
began with the earthly life of Christ would reach
its climax after a thousand years. Yet during the
subsequent centuries modifications had to be
made. Joachim[13] of Floris propounded the view

---

10. Although Augustine wrote no commentary on the Apocalypse,
he drew on it when writing his *De. Civ.* (cf. 20, 7ff). Cf. the
discussion on Augustine by G. Bonner, *Cambridge History of the
Bible* I, 554; G. Meier, *Die Johannesoffenbarung und die Kirche,*
Tübingen, 1981, 129–171. Meier shows some dependence of
Augustine on Tyconius.

11. His commentary is included in Migne, *P.G,* cvi.

12. His commentary is preserved in Migne, *P.L,* lxviii.

13. *Enchiridion in Apocalypsim.* For brief details see J. M. Court,
Myth and History, 7.

that the age in the immediate future would be the age of the Spirit, which lent support to the monastic ideal, for the Spirit was believed to favour contemplation. Joachim saw many contemporary historical events reflected in the Apocalypse. For him antichrist was the worldliness of the present church, but Joachim's followers soon arrived at the conclusion that antichrist was the Pope, a view which was later to find favour among the reformers. During the fourteenth century, another view emerged, advocated by Nicholas[14] of Lyra, who regarded the Apocalypse as portraying the whole sweep of church history from the foundation to the end of time in seven periods. It was in the fifth period that he saw many contemporary events, while the sixth period was seen as that of antichrist.

During the reformation period, as we have already noted, the most influential expositors bypass this book altogether. Where reference was made to it the idea of the Pope as antichrist seemed the most obvious conclusion. A Jesuit interpreter, Ribeira,[15] however, returned to the expositions of the early fathers for his understanding of the book. He regarded everything following the fifth seal as referring to the endtime, a strictly eschatological interpretation. Another Jesuit, Alcasar,[16] saw the main part of the book as dealing with the conflict of the church with Judaism (5–11) and with paganism (12–19). Hence the book does not go beyond the time of Constantine in its predictions. This writer may be regarded as a precursor of attempts to produce an

---

14. For details, see H. B. Swete, *op. cit.*, ccix.
15. *Commentarius in sacram b. Ioannis Apoc*, Salamanca, 1591.
16. *Vestigatio arcani sensus in Apoc*, Antwerp, 1614.

interpretation of the book which treats it as a whole.[17]

When we reach the period of the development of historical criticism, we note certain other influences entering into the process of interpretation. Study of Jewish apocalyptic literature shows many similarities between this literature and our apocalypse. The book began to be set against the background of its literary genre, which meant that many of the earlier approaches were seen to be unsatisfactory. It was assumed that the readers of the Apocalypse of John would have the same approach as the readers of the widely circulating Jewish apocalypses. One of the foremost exponents of this view was R. H. Charles, whose commentary in the International Critical Commentary series was based on the view that this book belonged to the genre of Jewish apocalyptic literature. Yet more recent scholarship has pointed out many differences between our apocalypse and those of the Jewish writers, and this has necessitated a reassessment of Charles's position.[18]

Whereas comparison with Jewish apocalypses has yielded many useful insights, yet the differences are considerable. Ellul regards the transmutation of the genre[19] as so extensive that he

---

17. Many modern interpreters have followed similar principles of interpetation. Cf. W. Ramsay, *The Letters to the seven Churches of Asia and their place in the plan of the Apocalypse,* London 1904. L. Giet, *L'Apocalypse et l'Histoire,* Paris 1957, also adhered to a strictly contemporary method of interpeting and dating the book. In commenting on Giet's method, Court, *op cit.,* 13, remarks that points of contact with persecution are too sparse.
18. See C. Rowland, *The Open Heaven,* London 1982, 191ff., for such a reassessment. See also the discussion of J. Kallas, 'The Apocalypse—An Apocalyptic Book?,' *JBL* 76, 1967, 69–80, and J. Ellul, *L'Apocalypse, architecture en mouvement,* Paris 1975. Eng. tr. G. W. Schreiner, *The Apocalypse,* New York 1977, 9ff.
19. *Op. cit.,* 30.

does not hold that this book can be interpreted as 'an instance of apocalypse'. The major distinction is that the Apocalypse of John does not stand by itself: it is indeed called 'the revelation of Jesus Christ' and John himself is no more than the channel through whom it is transmitted. In this connection it must be recognized that this book lacks the resort to pseudonymity[20] almost invariably found in the Jewish works; it does not review past history; and its message is predominantly optimistic. In view of this we must recognize the uniqueness of John's Apocalypse. According to Ellul it is essentially concerned with the present in its impact upon its readers.[21]

Some scholars during the last century adopted the view that most of this book is concerned only with the future and has nothing to do either with the original readers or with the intervening history of the church. This switch away from any form of historicizing interpretation had some influence on the development of such movements as dispensationalism.[22]

---

20. J. J. Collins, 'Pseudonymity, Historical Reviews and the Genre of the Apocalypse of John', *CBQ* 39, 1977, 329–343, considers the differences between Jewish apocalypses and John's to be superficial. E. S. Fiorenza, *The Book of Revelation, Justice and Judgment*, 1985, 10 n. 6, disagrees with Collins. C. Rowland, *op. cit.*, 69, considers that the reason why pseudonymity was not a prominent feature in Christian apocalypses was that the necessity for it ceased with the coming of the Spirit.

21. *Op. cit.*, 24. Some scholars have argued strongly that the Book of Revelation should be regarded as prophecy (cf. D. Hill, 'Prophecy and Prophets in the Revelation of St. John', *NTS* 18, 1972, 401–418; *idem New Testament Prophecy*, London 1979, 70–93.

22. Cf. the position adopted by such writers as J. D. Pentecost, *Things to Come*, Grand Rapids 1964; J. F. Walvoord, *The Millenial Kingdom*, Findlay Ohio 2nd edition 1963; C. Ryrie, *Dispensationalism Today*, Chicago 1965.

The Problem of Sources

Most characteristic of the historical-critical method has been the concentration on sources. It is considered that in order to discover what an author wants to say some examination of the sources used by him is imperative. If we can establish how a writer has utilised the material available to him we can discover more readily what was in his mind.[23] The theory is undoubtedly reasonable. But the nineteenth and early twentieth centuries were cluttered with so many different theories about possible sources as to undermine the possibility of establishing any certainty, so great has been the diversity.[24]

We may note the three main types of sources which have been proposed. The first type is pagan material of a mythical kind, as for instance the view that dragon mythology lies behind Revelation 12.[25] The second type suggested is material said to

---

23. Cf. W. G. Kümmel, *Introduction to the New Testament,* Eng. tr. London 1966, 332.

24. For a survey of the theories current in the nineteenth century, cf. J. Moffatt, *Introduction to the Literature of the New Testament,* 3rd edit. 1918, 489f. See also G. Meier, *Johannesoffenbarung,* 448ff.

25. See P. Prigent, *Apokalypse 12,* Tübingen 1959, for a survey of theories on this chapter. Some have appealed to Greek mythology (A. Dieterich, *Abraxas. Studien zur Religionsgeschichte des spätern Altertumsn,* Leipzig, 1891, 117ff). Others have seen parallels with Babylonian mythology (H. Gunkel, *Schöpfung und Chaos in Urzeit und Endzeit. Eine religionsgeschichtliche Untersuchung über Gen 1 und Apoc 12,* Göttingen 1895, 171–398). W. Bousset, *Die Offenbarung Johannis,* Göttingen 1896, 354ff, appealed more to Egyptian and Iranian mythology, while F. Boll, *Aus der Offenbarung Johannis: Hellenistische Studien zum Weltbild der Apokalypse,* Leipzig-Berlin 1914, saw a mixture of both Babylonian ideas and Graeco-Roman developments. G. R. Beasley-Murray, *The Book of Revelation,* London 1974, 192, says there is wide argeement that we have here a Jewish-Christian adaptation of an international myth, which cannot be traced to any one source.

have originated as Jewish apocalyptic, which has been Christianized, but none too thoroughly.[26] The third is material taken by the author from the Old Testament. Of these theories the first and second have much less support than the third, although they still have some advocates.

The influence of the Old Testament on this book is undeniable. But various proposals in this connection have focused on different Old Testament books. The two main sources are undoubtedly Ezekiel and Daniel, both of which use similar types of imagery. That Ezekiel was the dominant influence has been maintained by A. Vanhoye,[27] but there has been rather more support for the view that Daniel was the major influence on the structure and theology of the book. Recently G. K. Beale[28] has devoted a monograph to the task of demonstrating the strong use of Daniel in this book. Further support for Daniel as a main source may be seen in the work of Austin Farrer[29] and J. P. M. Sweet.[30] Beale points out the significant use of Dan. 2:28–29, 45 in introducing four major sections (1:1; 1:19; 4:1; 22:6). Some use of Daniel and other Old Testament books such as Ezekiel

---

26. So E. Vischer, 'Die Offenbarung Johannis: eine jüdische Apokalypse in christlicher Bearbeitung', *Texte und Untersuchungen* 1886, 35–46. A mediating view is that which sees the book as a combination of a Jewish work (4:1–22:7) and Christian work (1:1–3:22, 22:8–21). This has been recently advocated by J. F. Whealon, 'New patches on an Old Garment: the Book of Revelation', *Biblical Theology Bulletin* 11, 1981, 54. He claims to find an absence of specifically Christian concepts and values in the Jewish part.
27. 'L'utilization du livre d'Ezechiel dans l'Apocalypse', *Biblica* 43, 1962, 436–472.
28. *The Use of Daniel in Jewish Apocalyptic Literature and in the Book of Revelation*, University Press of America 1984.
29. *The Revelation of St. John the Divine*, Oxford 1964.
30. *Revelation*, London 1979, 17ff.

and Zechariah must be conceded.[31] But does this amount to the use of literary sources?

May not the explanation be that the author's mind was saturated with the Old Testament to such an extent that he was not conscious of following any particular sources? Such a view will still make it imperative to examine the Old Testament background so as to recognize the rich mental images with which his mind was stocked and by means of which the patchwork of ideas in this book are expressed. Yet we must be even more concerned to discover how best to analyze its structure and to decipher its many symbols.

The Problem of the Structure

Some may feel that the structure of the book is unimportant for determining its message. But it has been generally recognized that to discover an author's purpose it is essential to formulate some notion of the scheme underlying his work. Otherwise there is danger of isolating statements from their context and thus distorting meaning. In the case of the book of Revelation there is however no consensus over structure, apart from the easily observed fact that there are at least four series of sevens. We might almost say that there are as many proposals as proposers. No other New Testament book has been subjected to so many theories. We cannot assume that it is possible to arrive at a definitive position.

---

31. For a recent study of the use of the Old Testament in the Apocalypse, cf. F. Jenkins, *The Old Testament in the Book of Revelation,* Grand Rapids, 1976.

The Prologue and Epilogue

There are at least some agreed propositions. Most would accept that the book has a prologue and epilogue. The prologue consists at least of 1:1–3. Some would also conclude 1:4–8.[32] Some even add verses 9–20. The epilogue is generally thought to begin with 22:6ff.[33] But some take it from 22:10.[34] Various starting points have been suggested for the remaining section. The main problems are whether the letters-section is integral with the rest, and whether the visions are continuous or recapitulatory. In view of the mention of the churches in 22:16, it is reasonable to suppose that the whole section was intended as a complete structure. Some, especially dispensationists, make a division at 4:1, and impose a different interpretation on each part.[35]

Recapitulation or Continuation?

It was the ancient assumption (supported by Victorinus and Augustine) that the series of judgments, represented by the seals, trumpets and bowls, should be regarded as parallels and therefore the second and third series are recapitulatory. This view has many modern advocates.

The main argument in support of the opposing view that each series follows on from the preceding one is the fact that the seventh seal and seventh

---

32. Cf. F. Hahn, 'Zum Aufbau der Johannesoffenbarung', in *Kirche und Bibel,* Paderborn 1979, 145–154.
33. Cf. J. Lambrecht, 'A Structuration of Revelation 4, 1–22, 5' in *L'Apocalypse johannique et l'Apocalyptique dans le Nouveau Testament,* 1980, 77–104.
34. Cf. C. H. Giblin, 'Structural and Thematic Correlations in the Theology of Revelation 16–22', *Biblica* 55, 1974, 487–504.
35. See R. H. Mounce, *The Book of Revelation,* Grand Rapids 1977, 82, for a discussion of the threefold formula in 1:11 in support of this.

trumpet both lead into the next sequence. But the chief difficulty is the repetition at the close of each series of the approaching end. Many sections also appear to interrupt the supposed progress (e.g. 7, 10–11, 12–14).[36] The joins which link the parts together are alleged to support a continuation theory.

Whatever the choice between these theories, there are certain issues which any proposed solution must explain. (a) What is the relation between the letters and the visions? (b) What is the relationship between history and theology? (c) What is the significance of the hymns? (d) What is the significance of the number seven? These issues are in addition to the more fundamental one of the interpretation of the many symbols. Arising from this is the question of the relation of the book to the Old Testament.

Various Proposals

No attempt to classify theories is entirely adequate, but the value of getting an overall idea of current suggestions lies in the caution it inspires against the temptation to adopt an over-facile approach.

An Editing of Various Sources
In the era when source criticism was at its height, the whole New Testament was approached from the point of view of editing. The idea of development was irrelevant, for the editor was too tied to his sources.[37] But interest in theories of sources

---

36. E. S. Fiorenza, 'Composition and Structure of the Apocalypse', *CBQ* 39, 1977, 362, (reprinted in her book *The Book of Revelation, Justice and Judgment*, Philadelphia 1985, 172ff) refers to the presence of intercalation.
37. For such theories, see J. Moffatt, *op. cit.*, 491.

has slackened. Boismard's theory that an editor has combined two sets of visions—one in Nero's time and the other in Vespasian's or Domitian's time—has not been taken up.[38] Another view is that the author has subjected his various traditions to successive editorial processes.[39] This would make it more feasible to maintain the linguistic unity of the book, but does not explain the unity of its composition.[40]

Poetic Imagery Theory

If the author was a visionary or a poet, it is useless to look for a previously thought-out development.[41] There is much to be said for this kind of impressionistic view, for it dispenses with chronology altogether, and responds to the overall impact rather than searching for a continuing development.

Symbolism

There can be few interpreters who do not agree that there is symbolism in the book. But Farrer has systematically attempted to explain the whole structure thus.[42] He suggested three symbolical keys—the number seven, the Jewish liturgy, and astrology (the signs of the zodiac). But to maintain the theory there is much manipulation of evidence, and it needs to be asked whether the readers would have grasped the symbolism. As an

---

38. Cf. *RB* 56, 1949, 507–539. For details of the two sets of visions, see the *Jerusalem Bible, New Testament,* 429. Boismard concluded that chs. 1–3 originally existed as a separate text.

39. This is the position adopted by H. Kraft in his commentary, *Die Offenbarung des Johannes,* 1974.

40. Note the criticism by E. S. Fiorenza, *CBQ* 39, 1972, 350.

41. Cf. M. Kiddle, *The Revelation of St. John,* London 1940.

42. *A Rebirth of Images,* Westminster 1949, and *The Revelation of St. John the Divine,* Oxford 1964.

explanation of the structure of the book Farrer's theory is not convincing for it introduces too much subjectivity.

Drama

Several scholars have suggested that the book has been arranged after the pattern of a dramatic presentation. J. W. Bowman[43] argued that the whole book was constructed on the pattern of Greek dramatic productions. The connecting sections were seen as stage props for the different acts. Only 1:1–4 and 22:21 were thought to have been appended later. The various angelic directions are compared with the use of gods in Greek plays.

Prior to Bowman, R. R. Brewer[44] had argued for the influence of Greek drama on Revelation, particularly with regard to the chorus. Still earlier E. W. Benson[45] had compared the hymns to the chorus of Greek drama. Recently J. L. Blevens[46] has revived the appeal to Greek drama.

But the book of Revelation differs from Greek plays by being far less of a dialogue. Moreover there is no interchange between the hymns and the dialogue as in Greek plays. It lacks the kind of discussion which occurs in Greek plays when the chorus debates what action is advisable. Yet it must be admitted that the hymns, like the Greek chorus, have an interpretive function.[47]

---

43. 'The Revelation of John: its dramatic Structure and Message', *Interpretation* 9, 1955, 436–453.
44. *ATR* 18, 1936, 71–92.
45. *The Apocalypse: Structure and Principles of Interpretation*, London 1900, 37ff.
46. 'The Genre of Revelation', *Review and Expositor* 17, 1980, 393–408.
47. Cf. G. Delling, 'Zum gottesdienstlichen Stil der Johannesapikalypse', *NovT* 3, 1957, 107–137.

Sevenfold Structure

Most theories have some reference to the significance of seven, but the following base the whole structure on groupings of seven. We note first the theory advanced by R. L. Loenertz[48] that there are seven groups of seven. In addition to the letters, seals, trumpets and bowls, the rest is also divided into sevens. J. W. Bowman also has a sevenfold division for his dramatic theory.[49] Lohmeyer[50] went further and created subdivisions also consisting of sevens. This theory appears artificial, for it is difficult to imagine a prophet producing work so intricately structured.

More recently, A. Yarbro Collins[50] has proposed the following scheme:

(1) Prologue	(5) Seven unnumbered visions
(2) Seven messages	(6) Seven bowls
(3) Seven seals	(7) Seven unnumbered visions
(4) Seven trumpets	(8) Epilogue

By postulating two unnumbered series, this theory proposes a structure of six sevens. But it also depends on two appendices, a Babylon Appendix following (6) and a Jerusalem Appendix following (7). But it may be asked why an author who was so fascinated by numbers included two unnumbered series.

Liturgical

Because of the inclusion of hymns, several theories begin with these in suggesting a structure for the whole book. One theory finds a paschal liturgy as the basis. Massey Shepherd[51] takes the five parts

---

48. Cf. R. J. Loenertz, *The Apocalypse of St. John* (Eng. tr. H. J. Carpenter) London 1947.

49. Cf. Spink's critique in *EQ* 50, 1978.

50. *The Combat Myth in the Book of Revelation*, Missoula 1976.

51. *The Pashcal Liturgy and the Apocalypse*, London 1960.

of the Paschal Vigil and relates them to the book of Revelation in the following way.

Scrutinies (1–3)	Synaxis (8–19)
Vigil(4–6)	Eucharist (19–22)
Initiation (7)	

However the evidence for the liturgy which Shepherd uses is much later, and no dependence can be placed on it.

S. Läuchli[52] also argues for a eucharistic sequence in the hymn sections. He thinks the use of these hymns in sequence points to the Eucharist as observed in Ephesus. This involves an editorial theory in which the visions are superimposed on the liturgical framework. Yet another approach takes as its starting point the influence of the Jewish synagogue service.[53]

Concentric Theory
There has been some support for a sevenfold division in which the fourth section is seen as the pivot with the other sections leading up to and away from it. So there is correspondence between the various stages as the following table shows—

```
         (A)  1:1–8
            (B)  1:9–3:22
               (C)  4:1–9:21 & 11:15–19
                  (D)  10:1–15:4
               (C')  15:5–19:10
            (B')  19:11–22:9
         (A')  22:10–21
```

---

52. 'Eine Gottesdienststruktur in der Johannesoffenbarung', *ThZ* 16, 1960, 359–378.
53. Cf. L. Mowry, 'Revelation 4–5 and Early Christian Liturgical Usage', *JBL* 71, 1952, 75–84. This study is restricted, however, because it deals with only part of the evidence. K-P Jörns, *Das hymnische Evangelium, Untersuchungen zu Aufbau, Funktion und Herkunst der hymnischen Stücke in der Johannesoffenbarung,*

This has been advocated by E. S. Fiorenza,[54] but the connections between AA', BB', and CC' are not easy to demonstrate.

Historical-prophetic Theory

Recently a treatment has appeared which interprets the whole book as pointing towards the first advent of Christ not the second. E. Corsini[55] sticks to the four sevens for his major divisions, and treats chs. 12–14 as recalling and deepening the messages of the letters, seals and trumpets; ch. 12 as relating to the creation and fall of man; ch. 13 as pointing to the corruption of political and religious authority; ch. 14 as referring to the Old economy as the first salvific intervention. Then chs. 17–19:10 deal with the death of Christ as judgment on history; chs. 19:11–20:15 with the death of Christ as the final destruction of evil forces; and chs. 21:1–22:5 with the death of Christ and the heavenly Jerusalem. The section 22:6–21 is regarded as an epilogue corresponding to 1:1–8 as the Proemium. This is certainly an original theory which differs totally from almost all its competitors in refusing to see any reference to the second coming.

Historical-apocalyptic View

An attempt has been made to differentiate between the first half of the book (1–11) as historical because

---

Gütersloh 1971, rejects the liturgical structure hypothesis, but sees the hymns as containing the gospel. He has been criticized by T. Holtz, *TLZ* 97, 1972, 358–360, for confining the gospel to the hymns.

54. 'Composition and Structure of the Apocalypse', *CBQ* 39, 1977, 344–366, reprinted in *The Book of Revelation. Justice and Judgment,* 159–180.

55. *Apocalisse prima e dopo,* Turin, Eng. tr. *The Apocalypse,* Wilmington 1983.

it shows the church's triumph over Judaism, and the second half (12–22) as projecting into the future to portray the impending judgments of God on Rome.[56] It is supposed that this combination of past history and future prediction is wholly in line with the nature of apocalyptic. But it is not clear why the seals and trumpets relate to the past while the bowls relate to the future.

Dialectical Arrangement

J. Ellul[57] sees five septenaries—churches, seals, trumpets, bowls and visions introduced with the formula, 'Then I saw'. He appeals to many contrasts in support of his dialectical theory—e.g. the slaughtered lamb and the raised lamb, the people of Israel (a fixed number) and the people of the nations (limitless).

There is no doubt some element of truth in a number of these theories, but whoever is searching for the meaning of the book as a whole finds himself faced by a bewildering choice with little means of testing which view is correct. The very proliferation of such theories is a sufficient reminder that any dogmatism on the matter is entirely out of place.

The Problem of Symbols

In our brief survey of the history of interpretation we have already noted the fundamental difference between those who interpreted the book literally and those who interpreted it spiritually. The tension between these two schools of thought still dominates twentieth century quests for the mean-

---

56. Cf. M. Hopkins, 'The Historical Perspective of Apocalypse 1–11', *CBQ* 27, 1965, 42–47.
57. *The Apocalypse,* New York 1977.

ing of this book. The fact is that the division between these approaches is too sharply drawn to be useful. It is equally impossible to treat the whole as symbolic, as it is to regard the whole book as being intended literally. Some of the imagery is so fantastic that it cannot bear a literal sense, as for instance the description of the locusts. Some element of symbolism must be admitted. But the literalists are understandably wary because of the lack of agreement on the meaning of the symbols.

There are some important questions which arise here. Why did the writer use such figurative language? How did he expect his readers to understand what he had written? Is it possible now to recapture the meaning? If the answer to the last question is in the negative, we should have to conclude that the book of Revelation has no relevance now and we might as well have the courage to exclude it from the canon. Yet, while appreciating the great caution needed in treating this book as symbolic, we would suggest that to fail to do so would be inconsistent with a true exegetical approach. Certainly the original readers would have been more used than we are to symbolism, and it is reasonable to suppose that when the book was produced it was intended to be intelligible. As to why the writer used such obscure language, the most likely answer is that only by such means could he express these profound mysteries which he wished to pass on to his readers

Can we enunciate any principles of interpretation which will enable us to handle the symbolism with confidence, and therefore more readily discover whether the book has any present relevance? It is worth attempting, although in doing so we run the risk of oversimplifying. The first principle would seem to be that where there is any parallel use of the imagery in the Old Testament, we may reasonably expect to find some indication of meaning through a comparison of the use in this book with the use in the Old Testament. This may set us along the right lines, although it may not provide a conclusive answer, for the simple reason that the context may show the symbol to have been used in a different way. We must guard against the danger of supposing that parallels must give similar meanings.[58] Thus if the Old Testament imagery of the dragon is brought into our apocalypse we must allow for the possibility that it has been used with an entirely different meaning. At the same time, because the vision of Christ in ch. 1 has white hair reminiscent of Daniel's Ancient of Days, we must reckon with the possibility that this was intended to invest the Christ vision with aspects of deity.

The second principle of interpretation of symbol is that detail is likely to be unimportant. If we are intent on assigning meaning to every part of the figure we may be blurring the essential point that the text is aiming to make. It may be less important to decide the precise meaning of the scroll which the Lamb alone is worthy to open, than to concentrate on the unique worthiness of the Lamb. The text itself gives no indication of the contents of the scroll. The absence of such indication could be a clue to us to seek out the overall thrust of the passage rather than focus on the detail.

Another important principle in the interpreta-

---

58. D. Ezell, *Revelations on Revelation. New Sounds from old Symbols,* Waco 1977. He stresses that the cross/resurrection occasioned important changes in the significance of the symbols.

tion of the symbols is that we must take into account the author's purpose. If we suppose that the book is more like an artist's attempt to record his impressions than an attempt to represent precisely what he had seen, we shall be less likely to distort the meaning. Anyone looking at a surrealist painting and trying to interpret it in the same way as a representative painting will not only be totally unable to make any sense of it, but will entirely fail to appreciate what the artist was trying to do. This analogy admittedly fails because it may turn out that the artist was not attempting to communicate at all, but was simply giving vent to his own feelings. The writer of the Apocalypse, however, cannot be accused of this, for he clearly supposes that when the book is read out the hearers will expect to grasp what he is saying. This involves us in assuming as a principle of interpretation that each symbol has an intelligible meaning.

Yet a fourth principle is that of coherence. It is not sufficient to interpret each symbol on its own merits, any more than we can get a true appreciation of a jigsaw by minutely examining one piece. Each symbol has meaning only when seen as part of the whole. The dragon symbol, for example, needs to be set in the context of the conflict motif throughout the book.

Any theory which is selective is inadequate as a key to meaning in a book like this. It is not satisfactory for that reason to begin with the identification of the Beast as some of the medieval exegetes did, nor with the millenium as some modern exponents do. The interpretation of the symbol will remain an insoluble problem if piecemeal approaches to meaning are adopted.

We may add as a fifth principle that the

meaning of the symbol is always more than the symbol itself.[59] By their nature symbols hide, and what they hide can be surmised only through the attempt to identify them. This means that the value of the symbol is not always to be found in precise definitions of meaning.[60] The symbolic representation in the opening vision of Christ in ch. 1, for instance, cannot be reduced to straight-forward ordinary language without loss. It is the richness of the symbolic language, rendered more accessible by the insights into its meaning which the exegete can provide, which make up the total impact.

Is it possible to find any modern analogies to the use of such symbolism? G. R. Beasley-Murray[61] has suggested the political cartoon as an analogy. He cites the common use of animals to represent countries, as the lion for Britain, the eagle for the USA, and the bear for Russia. He thinks the use of caricature would have been immediately under-stood by the original readers. The difficulty of the modern interpreter is that he does not know the background to all the images used, although it is certain that many of them would have been familiar to the readers.

Conclusion

The most obvious implication from this brief sur-vey of the quest for meaning in Revelation is that

59. See Ellul's discussion, *op. cit.,* 33–35.
60. E.S. Fiorenza, *The Book of Revelation,* 186, maintains that if apocalyptic language is understood as poetic language, it would mean that the language would evoke rather than define meanings and this would enhance its value.
61. *The Book of Revelation,* London 1974, 16, 17.

the quest must go on. The mass of literature which continues to be devoted to this baffling book does not suggest that it is without relevance for to-day. In our succeeding studies we shall concentrate on some of the most relevant features of the book. But for the present we may be thankful that its abiding worth has not been lost simply because it has proved too difficult to decipher. Its treasures are there, but the faint-hearted will never find them. The further we go along this treasure quest the richer we shall become, but it may be necessary to discard some long cherished ideas on the way. This book is infinitely more than a puzzle enabling us to map out the events of the future. It is essentially a communication from God for those who have ears to listen. One of the greatest qualities needed by the investigators of Revelation is openness of mind.

*The Christology and its
Modern Challenge*

CHAPTER TWO

The Christology and its Modern Challenge

Before investigating the christology of this book, we must discuss the claim by some scholars that the whole book is more Jewish than Christian. No one would assert that it has no christology at all, but if the christological references are approached from the standpoint that the book is either not Christian or at best is so only in a diluted state, the christological quest would hardly be worthwhile and would certainly not provide any relevance for the modern christological debate. The attitude of the leading Reformers does not offer much confidence that any useful contribution may be found here. Luther relegated the book to a minor place in the canon because he could not find Christ in it. It was for this reason he regarded the book as a dumb prophecy, having nothing to say to him. Calvin was more restrained, but as we have already noted he never wrote a commentary on the book, as he did on almost all the New Testament books.

Many modern scholars have aligned themselves with Luther in judging the christology to be so far below that of the rest of the New Testament as to be negligible. C. H. Dodd's comment is worth repeating in this respect:

'The God of the Apocalypse can hardly be recognized as the Father of our Lord Jesus Christ, nor has the fierce Messiah, whose warriors ride in blood up to their horses' bridles, many traits that could recall Him of whom the primitive *kerygma* proclaimed that He went about doing good and healing all who were oppressed by the devil because God was with Him.'[1]

The book did not appeal to the existentialism of R. Bultmann who regarded it as a weakly Christianized Judaism.[2] One of the points he made was that *pistis* is used in a Jewish and not a Christian sense. To him this book accepts the present as a temporary time of waiting rather than as a moment of decision.

A recent approach to the christology of this book which draws a sharp division between the alleged Jewish and Christian parts of the book ends with a very different christology from that gained by approaching the book as a whole.[3] But a methodology which begins with assumptions about the Jewishness of the main apocalyptic section and then refuses to see those titles used in that section as applicable to Jesus is open to challenge. For instance the refusal to identify the Lamb with Jesus and the claim that it is used in a wholly Jewish sense, reduces dramatically the thrust of the whole, which thus becomes a combination of

1. *The Apostolic Preaching and its Development,* 3rd edition, London 1963, 49.

2. *Theology of the New Testament,* II, London 1955, 175.

3. Cf. Sarah A. Edwards, 'Christological Perspectives in the Book of Revelation' in *Christological Perspectives,* edited R. F. Berkey and S. A. Edwards, New York 1982, 139–154.

Jewish eschatological hopes and Hellenistic Jewish Christianity. There are, however, strong linguistic and theological reasons for maintaining the unity of the book. Another kindred approach is that which maintains that the christology supports a two-document theory.[4]

But are these estimates of the book's low Christian profile valid? An examination of the christology will go some way towards demonstrating that they are not.[5]

Our method of approach will be to examine (1) the visual representations of Christ in this book; (2) the various titles used of him; and (3) the functions ascribed to him. On the basis of these studies we shall then be in a position to judge to what extent the christology of this book is in line with that presented elsewhere in the New Testament, what are its distinctive features and how far any of it is relevant for modern theology.

It must at once be admitted that a first reading of the Apocalypse gives the impression of a different kind of christology which bears little resemblance to what is encountered in the gospels and epistles. But first impressions can be misleading, and in this case frequently result in wrong conclusions. The visions are a different form of communication from that used in the other books. Nowhere else do we find exalted descriptions, as

---

4. This view is adopted by J. Massyngbaerde Ford, *Revelation* 1975, in the Anchor Bible. This author argues for two Jewish apocalypses from John the Baptist and from his school. The redactor is seen as a Christian disciple of John. The theory has been criticized by E. S. Fiorenza on the grounds of the strong linguistic unity of the book, *CBQ* 39, 1977, 347.

5. Cf. the brief discussion by G. R. Beasley-Murray, 'How Christian is the Book of Revelation?' in *Reconciliation and Hope. Essays presented to L. L. Morris,* (ed. R. J. Banks, Grand Rapids/ Exeter 1974) 275–284.

distinct from exalted affirmations, of the risen
Christ. But this in itself partly explains the difference. The Apocalypse differs from the gospels
in concentrating on the post-resurrection period
rather than the earthly life of Jesus. It differs
from the epistles in that it is relating its christology
to the end-times rather than concentrating on
Christ in the life of the Christian communities.
Yet in comparing the Apocalypse with the gospels,
it must be recognized that the basis of the
presentation of Christ in the Apocalypse is of an
exalted person who has already accomplished his
mission in the sphere of history, and in the case of
the epistles it must be realized that many parallels
exist between the messages to the churches in
Revelation and the thrust of the New Testament
letters.

Visual Representations

The Vision in Chapter 1
It is significant that the first chapter is dominated
by a vision of one like a son of man in the midst
of the candlesticks. It is an imposing introduction, enhanced rather than complicated by the
highly symbolic language. Whatever the meaning
intended, no reader can fail to be struck by the
tremendous dignity of the account. John's record-
ing of his own reaction of overwhelming awe is
intended to evoke in every reader a similar
reaction (verse 17) and at the same time to give an
immediate assurance of the comfort and encouragement of the Risen Christ.
    The long robe and the golden girdle speak of
dignity, for the girdle around the breast suggests
a noble bearing and work completed, unlike the

workman's girdle around the loins. This hint of accomplishment will be expanded later, but for the time being it is the dignity of the person that is in mind. This emphasis is further enhanced by the description of his features. The whiteness of the hair and the blazing character of the eyes together build up a picture of one who is able to penetrate into men's minds in an authoritative way, the hair reminding us of the description of the Ancient of Days in Daniel's vision (Dan. 7:9). His assessment cannot be trifled with. The other features—the burnished bronze feet, the thunderous voice and the two-edged sword from the mouth—combine to impress on the reader the exalted appearance of the person seen. The additional descriptive note that his face shone like the sun is the only feature that bears any resemblance to the earthly Jesus, and even that only to the description of him in his transfigured form. As we gaze at the vision we cannot fail to be aware that it constitutes a hitherto unparalleled method of introducing the Jesus Christ who is making this revelation (1:1).

We may wonder why this means of communication has been selected here. We have discussed in our first study the implications of symbolism. But what advantage has the 'cartoon' method which makes it particularly appropriate here, rather than the more affirmative statements found elsewhere in the New Testament? A sufficient answer would be that since the visions of judgment could not be portrayed except by means of 'cartoons', this was regarded as the most appropriate way of introducing the Christological material. The readers are expected to look beyond the forms to the profound truth that this Christ is dignified yet approachable. The fact that he refers to his own

death and resurrection is in direct line with the
importance placed on that dual event in the rest of
the New Testament. We are faced with one who
has had a part in history ('I died') and who is
nevertheless now exalted ('I am alive for ever-
more'). The importance of the resurrection is seen
in the fact that Christ now has the keys of Death
and Hades (1:18). He has vanquished man's last
enemy, although the consummation of this victory
is not seen until the end of the book when Death
and Hades are cast into the lake of fire (20:14).

The Introductions to the Letters

This visual presentation of the book's christology
is extended and to some extent explained by the
descriptions of the one who gives the messages to
the seven churches. Most of them borrow from the
initial vision, but a few further details are added.
Christ has the seven spirits (3:1).[6] He is holy and
true and has the key of David (3:7). He is
described as the Amen, the faithful and true
witness, the beginning of God's creation (3:14).
The seven spirits are introduced in 1:4; the
character of holiness is seen in the refining fire;
the key of David is introduced because of the
reference to the synagogue of Satan in 3:9; the
faithful witness is from 1:5. But the Amen and the
arche[7] (beginning *or* first principle) are innova-
tions. The first reminds us of the use of 'Amen' in
the affirmations of Jesus and of the doxological

6. Cf. E. Schweizer, 'Die sieben Geister in der Apokalypse', *EvT*
11, 1951–52, 502–512; F. F. Bruce, 'The Spirit in the Apocalypse',
in *Christ and Spirit in the New Testament* (eds. B. Lindars and S. S.
Smalley, Cambridge 1973), 333–344.

7. G. Delling, *TDNT* I. 484, is not certain whether *arche* is used
here in the same sense as in Col. 1:18, but agrees that Rev. 21:6
and 22:13 point to that likelihood.

use of 'Amen' in 1:6,7, while the *arche* recalls Paul's use of it in Col. 1:18 in another profound Christological setting. But *arche* has also already been used of Christ in 1:5 in the sense of the ruler of kings on earth.

This building up of impressions of the immense dignity and significance of Jesus is clearly intended to underline the importance of the messages to the churches. There can be no doubt that the christology here is not theoretical but intensely practical. It is the exalted Christ who addresses his people. The descriptions are both encouraging and awe-inspiring. The one described holds the churches in his right hand yet nevertheless has a sharp sword and flashing eyes; he both commends and condemns. Yet there is nothing here to connect him with the human Jesus recorded in the gospels.

The Vision of the coming Judge in 14:14–16
Here is a description of one like a son of man seated on a cloud with a golden crown on his head and a sharp sickle in his hand. Since the expression 'one like a son of man' also occurs in 1:13, there can be no doubt that Christ is meant, in spite of the fact that verse 17 speaks of another angel with a sharp sickle. Here again we find what may at first appear to be a different concept of Christ from that found in the rest of the New Testament, but there are many New Testament references to Christ coming to judge as well as save, and this aspect of christology is necessary for a complete New Testament picture. Here is a royal harvester, fulfilling the predictions of Jesus himself in the parable involving an eschatological harvest (Mt. 13:30). The cloud imagery may be understood as echoing the language of Dan. 7:13, in which case it connects the one like a son of man here with the

Ancient of Days in Daniel, underlining again the exalted character of the book's christology.

The Vision of the Warrior King in 19:11–21

In this section the harvester image of ch. 14 is replaced by the more aggressive warrior imagery. The purpose of the coming is to judge and make war. There are no mitigating features, no saving possibilities. That there is intended to be a direct link with the vision in ch. 1 is clear from the description of the flaming eyes and the sword coming from the mouth. But other features take prominence: the many diadems; the robe dipped in blood; the mysterious name and the inscribed names—'The Word of God', 'King of Kings and Lord of Lords'. We have reached a revelation of Christ at the end of history. His saving work is done. His retinue is clad not in armour for battle, but in fine linen for a wedding. He acts only against those who are not numbered among his people. This representation is paradoxical. The imagery is martial but no battle ensues. The judgment is accomplished through a verbal sword. Christ has the last word at the consummation.[8]

In all these visual representations the figure of the exalted Christ is supreme. There is never any question concerning the issue. Victory is certain and is directly attributed to Christ himself. He performs precisely the function of God, a point which will be further enlarged on below. But before considering this, we must make a brief survey of the titles ascribed to Christ in this book.

---

8. S. A. Edwards, *Christological Perspectives,* 282 n.13, disagrees with G. Kittel, *TDNT* IV. 127, who identifies the Word of God here with Jesus. She thinks this warrior of the white anger of God is far removed from the Christ who prays, 'Father, forgive!' (p. 142).

Titles

'Jesus'

The name *'Jesus'* occurs sometimes on its own, sometimes linked with *'Christ'* and once with *'Lord'*. It will be worth noting the contexts in which these various uses occur, to discover whether each usage is theologically significant or whether it is merely stylistic.

In one case only *'Jesus'* is used to name the speaker. This is not until 22:16, and since it occurs in the concluding reference to the churches, it seems a parting reminder that the exalted one who addresses the churches is none other than the Jesus known from his earthly life. The other uses of the name 'Jesus' are all in the genitive. The 'faith of Jesus' (14:12) is clearly faith in Jesus. The 'martyrs of Jesus' (17:6) are those who have died for the sake of Jesus. The 'testimony of Jesus' (12:17; 19:10; 20:4) is the truth revealed by Jesus.[9] To these must be added the references to the Lord Jesus in the last two verses (22:20, 21).

The familiar title 'Jesus Christ' occurs only three times in this book, all in the first five verses (1:1, 2, 5). This is a form widely used throughout the book of Acts and the epistles and shows the way in which the early church incorporated the Messianic office into the proper name. There can be no disputing that for the Christian community Jesus was accepted as the Messiah expected by the Jewish people, although with a radical re-interpretation of the messianic office. That this most familiar title drops out of the book so soon seems

---

9. In order to maintain her theory that 'Jesus' does not occur in the apocalyptic section, Sarah Edwards, *Christological Perspectives* 149, is obliged to regard all these references as glosses. But there are no textual evidences for such a view, as she admits.

strange. Was it considered to be inadequate? It seems best to take this as an indication that the author attached considerable importance to the forms of titles he uses and that he prefers other names which have a stronger symbolic force.

'The Christ' (Ho Christos)

The form with the article occurs four times in this book and warrants careful attention because it is used as a designation rather than as a proper name. The passages are 11:15–19; 12:10–12; 20: 4–6 (where it occurs twice). A study of these passages[10] shows that in every case the designation is used in close proximity with 'Lord' (used of God) or 'God'. 'The Anointed' is used in texts dealing with the future reign of God in which he reigns through his annointed. The messianic function is therefore sublimated to the final reign, as contrasted with the present aspirations current among the contemporary Jews.[11]

The Lamb

Since this title occurs some 29 times in this book it must be reckoned to be the dominant conception of Christ. But what is the significance of the name? And why was it selected as the key to the author's christology?[12] It is difficult to escape from the

10. Cf. the article by M. de Jonge, 'The use of the expression Ho Christos in the Apocalypse of John', in *L'Apocalypse johannique et l'Apocalyptic dans le Nouveau Testament* (ed. J. Lambrecht), Leuven, 1980, 267–281.

11. This expression cannot, however, be understood only in a purely Jewish sense (cf. J. Massyngbaerde Ford, *Revelation,* New York 1975, 13–14), although it undoubtedly has Jewish undertones.

12. If, of course, the apocalyptic section is divorced from the Christian section (as it is by S. A. Edwards, *Christological Perspectives* 142ff), the Lamb ceases to be the key to the Christology of the whole book.

impression that the term is best understood against a Jewish background. Since lambs played such an important part in the Jewish sacrificial system, it is reasonable to suppose that the answer to our questions must be sought from such a source. The lamb was a key factor in the Old Testament view of atonement. When the lamb was sacrificed the worshipper was accepted before God.

The Lamb imagery as used in Revelation is also indebted to Jewish apocalyptic. The people of God are represented as God's flock, and the deliverer of the people is seen as a seven-horned lamb. In the Testament of Joseph 19:8f, the Messiah of Judah is represented as a lion and the Messiah of Aaron as a lamb, a combination highly significant for an understanding of the imagery in Rev. 5. The apocalyptist saw the lamb as a powerful conqueror, which suggests that the lamb symbolism had been swallowed up by the lion symbolism.[13] Indeed there is no suggestion that the lamb had to be sacrificed.

The Lamb of Revelation is no ordinary lamb. He is not one of a number; he is unique. He is introduced in 5:6 in the first heavenly worship scene.[14] It is clear that he shares the same worship as God does in ch. 4. The adoration of the heavenly choirs is addressed to the one on the throne and to the Lamb. There is no difference in their worthiness. But there are two highly significant features about the Lamb which at once come into view. The first is that he stands 'as though he

---

13. G. R. Beasley-Murray, *Revelation*, 125, comments that 'The warrior-Lamb then has conquered through accepting the role of the passover-Lamb'.
14. Cf. W. C. van Unnik, ' "Worthy is the Lamb", The Background of Rev. 5', in *Mélanges Beda Rigaux,* Gembloux 1970, 445–461.

had been slain'. The symbolism of this is beyond doubt. The wounding is the sacrificial act and the standing is the resurrection triumph. In view of the fact that little is said in Revelation about the work of Christ, it is of the highest importance that a slain-like Lamb stands over the whole book. The other intriguing feature is that this Lamb is first introduced as a lion, the Lion of the tribe of Judah. Although, as noted above, a lion-lamb imagery had been used previously in apocalyptic literature, its use here is unexpected because apparently contradictory in this context. Since the main theme of this book is the ultimate victory of God and Christ over the forces of darkness, we might have thought the Lion figure would have been more appropriate. But the Lion title occurs nowhere else in this book. Its appearance in 5:5 is a fleeting one, the idea of ferocity is swiftly replaced by the gentleness associated with the figure of the lamb. This suggests that the divine conquest will not be achieved by a display of might, as in the case of the lion-lamb in the Testament of Joseph, but by suffering and sacrifice. At the same time the many appearances of the Lamb in this book dispel any suggestion that the slain Lamb is anything but strong, well able to effect his conquering purposes.

We should note that various reasons have been advanced against the identification of the Lamb in the Apocalypse with the Lamb in Jn. 1:29, which is clearly seen to be Jesus. A different Greek word is used—*arnion* in Revelation and *amnos* in Jn. 1:29—but this verbal difference is not significant. It does not outweigh the remarkable fact that these two books use the same imagery in referring to Jesus' work of salvation (cf. Jn. 1:29 with Rev. 5:9). It is alleged that in the Apocalypse the Lamb symbolizes the people of Israel[15] on the assumption that this had become a standard apocalyptic convention. The identification with the sin-bearing Lamb of Jn. 1:29 is further thought to be christologically inappropriate because Revelation portrays the Lamb as sharing the throne of God. But a similar christology is found in the Epistle to the Hebrews and for that reason cannot be regarded as inappropriate.

There are some other significant features about the Lamb to be noted. He is the only one found worthy to open the book and it is he who initiates the series of judgments (see 6:1). The earthquake which follows the opening of the sixth seal is connected with the wrath of the Lamb. The gentle Lamb has given place to the judge, who strikes terror into the hearts of kings and generals and of the rich and strong. For this book the wrath of the Lamb is not a contradiction in terms and yet it is not the main characteristic of the Lamb.[16]

In the second worship passage, salvation is ascribed both to the Lamb and to the One on the throne (7:10). This is important because it offsets the impression that this book is concerned with judgment rather than salvation. The Christ of Revelation is the Saviour. The blood of the Lamb

---

15. Cf. S. A. Edwards, *Christological Perspectives,* 144; R. E. Brown, *The Gospel according to John,* Vol. I, New York 1966, 59.
16. R. H. Mounce, *The Book of Revelation,* Grand Rapids 1977, 163, has drawn attention to the fact that only once in the gospels is the word 'wrath' used of Jesus (Mk. 3:5). The term is not characteristic of the main portrait of the gospels. There would be less difficulty here, as Mounce points out, if the Lamb figure is messianic rather than sacrificial. A. T. Hanson, *The Wrath of the Lamb,* London 1957, 159–180, regards wrath as a process of retribution. For a full discussion of the wrath of God, cf. R. V. G. Tasker, *The Biblical Doctrine of the Wrath of God,* London 1951.

is mentioned not only in 5:9, but also in 7:14 and 12:11. The redemptive aspect is therefore prominent in this portrait of Christ. This book knows of no christology without the cross. It does not present the person of Christ apart from the work of Christ. This in itself is sufficient to caution against the view that the Lamb in Revelation is exclusively the warrior of God's wrath.

Another unexpected feature of the lamb imagery is the identification of the Lamb with the Shepherd in 7:17. He becomes the one who leads his people to springs of living water and the one who wipes away their tears. The shepherd is another theme which owes much to Old Testament usage (e.g. Ezek. 34, Ps. 23), but which also gains considerable significance for Christian readers through its use by Jesus of himself, in the Synoptic gospels as well as in John's gospel. Readers acquainted with the latter gospel would recognize that both the Lamb and Shepherd figures are combined in Jesus (cf. 1:29 and 10:1 ff). Since the shepherd passage in Revelation 7 is a prelude to the judgments following the blowing of the trumpets, the shepherd imagery is clearly intended to encourage the Christian readers.

The Lamb is seen as the keeper of the records, as is evident in the reference to the Lamb's book of life in 13:8. This links him with the destiny of his people, but also assures them that his purpose for them is to share the life that he himself possesses. The Lamb is further seen as the chief adversary of the forces of evil, for in the concluding outbursts of ferocity it is against him that the kings of the earth make war (17:14). He is in fact identified as Lord of lords and King of kings.

The centrality of the Lamb in this book is an important key to its structure and indeed to its interpretation.[17] The main theme of the book is thus seen to be encouragment and salvation rather than judgment.

Son of God

Once only is the title 'Son of God' used in this book (2:18, but the reference to 'my Father' occurs three times in the letters to the churches at 2:27; 3:5, 21). There are references to the Father in 1:6 and 14:1, both of which refer to God as Father of Christ. The immediate context of 2:18 suggests that this title may have been used because of its occurrence in Ps. 2:7–9, which is echoed in 2:27. But there is further supporting evidence indicating that the concept of Jesus as Son of God is an important feature in the christology of this book. It is worth observing that the status of sonship is reserved in the Apocalypse for Jesus Christ.[18] There is no hint that believers may also be called sons of God until 21:7 which is set in the New Jerusalem. This distinction may be thought to show a shift in emphasis compared with other parts of the New Testament, but Revelation is more intent on setting out the glorious standing of Christ and his certain victory than the relationship between him and believers, at least until the final consummation. Until then that relationship is adequately expressed by the idea of redemption.

---

17. Cf my article 'The Lamb in the Structure of the Book of Revelation', *Vox Evangelica* 12, 1981, 64–71. Cf also D. R. Carnegie's article, 'Worthy is the Lamb: The hymns in Revelation', in *Christ the Lord,* ed. H. H. Rowdon, Leicester 1982, 243–256.
18. E. Schweizer, *TDNT* 8, 389, considers that for the writer of Revelation 'Son of God' is to be understood only within the limits of Jewish understanding. But this seems an inadequate explanation of the reference in 2:18, the context of which cannot be regarded as Jewish.

The more intimate relationship which follows from this seems to be assumed.

Alpha and Omega

As a title Alpha and Omega is first introduced as the name for God in 1:8.[19] Since the first and last letters of the Greek alphabet are here used in conjunction with the descriptive 'who is and who was and who is to come' the reference must be to God as all-inclusive. He controls the whole of history, not just its beginning. This concept of God is significant in a book which looks ahead to the consummation of human history. It is underlined by the repetition of the title in 21:6. But what is most significant is that the same title is applied to Christ in 22:13. Some hint of it is found in 1:17 where the risen Christ introduces himself as 'the first and the last', an interpretation which is repeated in 22:13. The identification of both God and Christ by the same symbolic title is clearly intentional and is highly significant for our understanding of the christology of this book.

Word of God

When the warrior Christ appears in 19:11ff he bears the title, 'The Word of God'. It is not clear why this name is used here, but it seems most probable that if Christ were known as the Word, as he is in the prologue to John's gospel, the notion that he is the mediator of both the existing creation and of the new creation cannot be far from the writer's mind. It is generally supposed that the wisdom concept of Prov. 8 makes some contribution here. But probably the most impor-

---

19. Cf the note in G. R. Beasley-Murray's *Revelation,* 60–63, on the early Christian word-square which incorporated the Alpha and Omega symbol.

tant feature is the declaration in Jn. 1:1, that the Word was God, which underlies the concept in this context. Some distinguish here an echo from the Wisdom of Solomon 18:15–16, where the Word leaps from heaven carrying a sharp sword.[20] Yet while a striking parallel must be admitted, it is not sufficient for us to conclude that the concept here is totally Jewish rather than Christian. The concept of the Word of God as a sword is already found in Eph. 6:17 and Heb. 4:12.

The Functions of Christ in Revelation

In addition to the names ascribed to Christ, several functions which are normally asociated with God alone are referred to Christ in this book. We have already noted that the title Alpha and Omega is applied both to Christ and God. We have also observed that the background to the vision in chapter 1 is the Danielic Ancient of Days, which, in the passage from which the imagery is derived, is a name for God.

We may adduce several other similar characteristics. In the worship passages adoration is offered to the Lamb in the same way as it is offered to God. Moreover it is stated that both are worthy of worship and praise (4:11; 5:9,12). This may well be intended to counteract the cult of emperor worship which was developing and in which the emperor claimed the titles of Lord and God for himself. Even if this suggestion is correct, it would only serve to underline the significance of the attribution of worship to Christ, who unlike the emperor was thoroughly worthy to receive it. Certainly the word *axios* was not used in any

20. Cf. S. A. Edwards, *Christian Perspectives*, 142.

imperial declaration prior to the third century.[21]
In Rev. 5:13 and 7:10 the worship is in fact
addressed to him who sits on the throne and to the
Lamb—a joint act of homage which does not make
any real distinction between them as objects of
worship.

In 1:6 a doxology is addressed to Christ in the
same way as it would normally be addressed to
God. Moreover Christ shares the throne of God
(3:21; 22:1,3). In the New Jerusalem the water of
life flows from God and the Lamb (22:1). He is
described as 'the beginning of God's creation'
(3:14). The word used is *arche* and may be
understood in the sense of the one from whom
creation took its beginning.[22] The statement does
not therefore describe Christ as the first of God's
creation, an interpretation which in any case
would be out of keeping with the christology of
this book. It seems clear that 3:14 means that
Christ had a part in the creation of the world. In
view of the fact that in 4:11, creation is attributed
to God and the statement is made that all things
were created by God's will, the close cooperation of
Father and Son in the act of creation is but thinly
veiled.

In the New Jerusalem there is no need of any
light since both God and the Lamb are the source

---

21. Cf. K.-P. Jörns, *Das hymnische Evangelium* 56–73, for a full
discussion of this point. The view that *axios* related to the imperial
cult was advanced as long ago as 1926 by E. Peterson, *Heis Theos:
Epigraphische, formgeschichtliche Untersuchungen,* Göttingen
1926, 176–179. R. H. Mounce, 'Worthy is the Lamb', in *Scripture,
Tradition and Interpretation: Essays presented to Everett F.
Harrison* (ed. W. W. Gasque and W. LaSor, Grand Rapids 1978),
60–69, in commenting on this ascription maintains that no christology could be superior.
22. So I. T. Beckwith, *The Apocalypse of John,* London 1919,
reprinted Grand Rapids 1967, 488.

of illumination (21:23). Indeed, it would be true to say that the Lamb is capable of doing all that God does. We may well ask whether by stressing these features the author does not identify Christ with God to such an extent that their individual identity is lost. A survey of the full data for the christology of the Apocalypse shows clearly that the writer does not confuse the person of Christ with the person of God. There are passages in which the element of subordination occurs, and these must be set against the facts just mentioned.

The use of the father-son analogy as a means of expressing the relation between God and Christ implies that the Son is subordinate to the Father. He refers to God as his God (3:2,12). The power he has to rule has been received from God (2:27). The entire revelation which the book contains has been received from God. Behind the victorious activities of the Lamb is the supreme power and authority of God.

We must recognize that there is no attempt to reconcile these apparently contradictory concepts. But in this respect the book of Revelation is not exceptional. Yet because of the high christology of the book the tension is all the stronger. It is significant that in the New Jerusalem there is still a distinction between the Lamb and God, although their functions are so similar. The reference in 22:1 to the river flowing from the throne of God and of the Lamb uses a double preposition 'from' (*ek*) and this makes a clear distinction between them.

Relation to other New Testament Literature

Some attempt needs to be made by way of comparing the christology of Revelation into what is found in the rest of the New Testament. In what sense is the book parallel with and in what sense distinct from the other literature? There is little material which is sufficiently parallel with the Synoptic gospels. The most obvious feature is the amount of attention given to the passion of Christ, which provides a key to the significance of the slain Lamb of the book of Revelation. It is significant that the clearest indication of the meaning of the death of Christ in the Synoptic gospels, apart from the words of institution at the last supper, is the ransom passage in Mk. 10:45 and its Matthean parallel. The ransom imagery is used in Rev. 5:9 and some continuity with the teaching of Jesus in the Synoptic gospels is undeniable. Moreover the main name by which Jesus referred to his own mission, 'Son of Man', is at least echoed in the language of the vision in the opening chapter. It must also be noted that the Synoptic Jesus predicts an end time marked by wars and rumours of wars, a prophecy which finds an echo in this book. The apocalyptic sections in the Synoptic gospels bear a strong resemblance to the visions of conflict.[23]

The parallels between the christology of Revelation and that of the Fourth Gospel are more remarkable. In these two books occur the only instances of Christ being described under the figure of a lamb. Even if there is dispute over the background of the lamb imagery in Jn. 1:29 in that there is no mention of the lamb being slain, nevertheless the parallel imagery is striking. We

---

23. R. Bauckham, 'Synoptic Parousia Parables and the Apocalypse', *NTS* 23, 1977, 162–176, and L. A. Vos, *The Synoptic Tradition and the Apocalypse,* Kampen 1965, both study various parallels with the Synoptics and show how strong these are.

may also refer to the father-son relationship
which is prominent in John's gospel and finds
some echoes in Revelation. Further in these two
books Christ is described as Logos, although the
occurrence in Jn. 1:1 is the more remarkable.
Bearing in mind that the Logos title is not as
specifically found elsewhere in the New Testament, the proximity in christology between these
books is marked. Another point worth mentioning
is the use in Revelation of Amen as a description
of Christ. In view of the fact that John's gospel
uses the double Amen as an introduction to
important statements of Jesus, it is not unreason-
able to see this as another parallel between the
two books.

When the christology of Revelation is compared
with that of Acts, it at once becomes evident that
the former has a more advanced presentation. The
statement in Acts 2:36 that God had made Jesus
both Lord and Christ is nevertheless amply illus-
trated in the book of Revelation. Moreover, the
vision of Stephen when he saw Jesus standing at
the right hand of God surrounded by the glory of
God is in line with the exalted christology of
Revelation. Stephen described him as the Son of
Man, and this is reminiscent of the one like a son
of man who appears in the initial chapter of this
book. Another point worth noting is that the
redemptive work of Christ which finds expression
in Revelation also occurs in Acts, as for instance
in Acts 20:28 which affirms that God bought his
church with his own blood, a remarkable statement which would tally well with the slain Lamb
imagery in the Apocalypse.

Those who would write off the christology of this
book as inferior to that of Paul should consider a
number of significant parallels. The christology is

admittedly expressed in different terms but is nonetheless of a similar pattern. The use of *arche* in Col. 1:15 resembles that in Rev. 3:14, although Paul goes into considerable detail in enlarging on his view of Christ. The use of the father-son analogy of the relationship between Christ and God is widespread in Paul's writings and may be said to be an indispensable factor for a true appreciation of his christology. Whereas in Paul it is prominent and in Revelation rather less obvious, there would be no disagreement between them on the importance of seeing Christ as the Son of God.

Paul's idea of Christ delivering up the kingdom to the Father (1 Cor. 15:24) is seen to be fulfilled in the announcement of the seventh angel (Rev. 11:15). The eschatological aspect of the kingdom receives reinforcement in this book, and it is most likely that Paul would not have found the teaching about the consummation of the age alien to his own ideas. He was as convinced as the writer of Revelation that God is sovereign over his world.

Yet another feature which this book shares with the Pauline epistles is the conviction that a spiritual warfare is in progress in which the chief antagonist of Christ and his people is the devil. Paul speaks of the spiritual forces of evil in the heavenly realms (Eph. 6:12), which would provide an admirable backcloth for the conflict in the book of Revelation. Paul is convinced that Christ will put all his enemies under his feet (1 Cor. 15:25) and this is precisely what the Lamb does in this book.

We may also point out that Paul says no more about the earthly life of Jesus than is found in this book. Both writers seem to assume the historical facts without seeing any need to reiterate them. This suggests indeed that here was a policy followed among the earliest Christians, one which would be strengthened after the writing of the gospels.

In Paul's appeal to the Corinthians, he reminds them they all must appear before the judgment seat of Christ (2 Cor. 5:10). He sees Christ as Judge as well as Saviour. Some commentators draw a distinction between the judgment seat of Christ here and the great white throne of Rev. 20:11ff, on the ground that in the latter case the judge is God, but the distinction is not convincing in the light of what has been said above about the similar functions of God and Christ. There can be no disputing that Paul shares with Revelation a conviction of the dominant role of Christ in judgment at the consummation of this age. Enough has been said to show that the approach in this book would not be as incompatible with that of Paul as many imagine.

A comparison with the rest of the New Testament will show christological parallels. If the view of God in Revelation is thought to be fierce, we note that in Heb. 12:29 he is described as a consuming fire and yet in the same context the intermediary work of Christ is mentioned (verse 24). Although the concept of Christ's intercession for his people is absent from Revelation, his deep concern for them and protection of them is everywhere apparent. Moreover, the powerful effect of the blood of Christ in the development of the theme of Christ's high priesthood in Hebrews finds an echo in the references to the blood in Revelation. The same may be said of 1 Peter 1:18, where the redemption theme appears, and of 1 John 1:7 where it is the blood that purifies.[24]

---

24. Cf. A. M. Stibbs, *The Meaning of the Word 'Blood' in Scripture*, London 1947.

These brief comparisons are sufficient to show that this book finds many points of contact with the main documents of early Christianity. It stands well within the primitive traditions. It certainly presents its own form of christology, but the figure of Christ which it describes is recognizable as the Christ of the Gospels, Acts and Epistles. In view of this our concluding task will be to comment on the relevance of this book in the modern debates on christology.

Relation to Modern Christology

Since our aim has been to demonstrate the modern relevance of the Apocalypse, we must face the question of what part its christology may play in modern discussions. If we are simply repc   ng the present position we shall have to admit at once that the book of Revelation does not figure much in those discussions. This has largely been brought about by the poor opinion many theologians hold of the value of the presentation of Christ in this book. If Revelation is regarded as essentially sub-Christian then its christological witness can be ignored. But if its christology is of an exalted kind, as the evidence surveyed above suggests that it is, it cannot be overlooked.[25] It may be necessary to point out that the symbolism of the book should not be allowed to mask its presentation of theological truth, but no account of a complete New Testament theology can dispose of the clear evidence of this book.

---

25. Cf. T. Holtz, *Die Christologie der Apokalypse des Johannes*, Berlin 1971: K. M. Fischer, 'Die Christlichkeit der Offenbarung des Johannes', *TLZ*, 1981, 165–172.

The first question we need to ask is whether in view of its high christology this book may possibly be regarded as docetic in character. It must be admitted that the divine aspect is more prominent than the human. But does this mean that the christology is divorced from the human Jesus? This is a fair question. Yet the fact that the central feature of the book is the slain Lamb shows indisputably that an act which took place on earth in the human life of Jesus (his death) takes pride of place among the multifarious descriptions of future actions. The heavenly worshippers in ch. 5 focus on the redemptive significance of the 'blood' of the Lamb. No docetic interpretation would recognize this. It was the very fact that Jesus was alleged to have died that caused the docetists to affirm that the heavenly Christ withdrew from the earthly Jesus before the passion. The book of Revelation firmly roots its christology in history. The impressive presentation of Christ in the book must be placed against a historical background.

Another question is whether Revelation lends any support to the modern concept of a developing christology. Does this book, in fact, represent the end product of an extended process, affected by ideas of divine men drawn from Hellenistic sources? Those who are intent on searching for sources from which every aspect of the Christian concept of Christ could be derived, have no alternative but to regard the christology in this book as highly developed and belonging to the later stages of Christian speculation. But it is equally possible and equally valid to trace the exalted concepts found within this book to the experience of the resurrection of Christ. Would those who saw the risen Christ have found the description in ch. 1

alien? Is it necessary to suppose that the most primitive idea of Christ was far removed from the view presented in this book? He who had conquered death could conquer anything and the book bears testimony to this.

What must never be lost sight of is that the writer claims his book to be a revelation of Jesus Christ. He is convinced that it has not resulted from his own mind. He does not claim to have researched innumerable sources in order to present a more developed christology than had been previously conceived. He writes as if his descriptions of Christ will appear most natural to his readers, without needing any explanations. Insufficient credit is given to the strong possibility that this book arose out of the writer's own personal experience of the risen Christ. This after all is the way in which he purports to have received the revelation.

A third question is to what extent the christology of this book can have any relevance to the modern existential debate. It is not surprising that Bultmann[26] could find no place for Revelation in compiling his New Testament theology. If the main thrust of New Testament Christianity is the present and its challenge to decision, the exaggerated stress on the future in this book would seem at once to render it irrelevant. But it is impossible to excise the present from the Apocalypse. In fact it presents a remarkable blend of present and future. Christ addresses his messages to churches which exist in the present although in all of these challenges promises are made which relate to the future. It may in fact be claimed that this book, with its objective presentation of Christ, offers a

---

26. Cf. his *Theology of the New Testament*, Eng. tr. I 1952, II 1955.

strong corrective to the almost totally subjective christology of much existential theology. The enthroned Christ is far removed from a purely subjective experience of Christ. The former is in every way as necessary as the latter. Revelation presents Christ as Lord of history in a way which modern christology has largely lost. This leads to our fourth question.

We need to enquire what is the connection between christology and eschatology as presented in this book. That there is a vision of the kingdom of God which is glorious but future is undeniable. The New Jerusalem shines ahead as the hope for mankind. But this hope is of a very different kind from the expectation of the coming messianic kingdom nourished among the Jews, both from the Old Testament and from the apocalypses. And the reason for the difference is the character of the Messiah who is presented. Conqueror he may be, but his conquest is through an act of redemption, not through a military blow which would reduce the enemy to total weakness. Whatever is done is done by the slain Lamb. The Lamb's redemptive work lies in the past, not in the future. Its completed character removes all doubt about the final outcome. The future will see the acknowledgment by the whole world of the establishment of the kingdom of God. But the message of this book seems to be that the final triumph is implicit in the redemptive work already accomplished. It is for this reason that the slain lamb dominates the book.

Conclusion

A careful examination has shown that this book presents an exalted and reassuring picture of

Christ. We may wonder why Martin Luther did not discover it, and why so many others have neglected it. It is to be hoped that many more, who have perhaps been frightened off by the somewhat strange and at times even lurid imagery, will explore again its magnificent view of Christ and will take heart from its unshakeable conviction that the Lamb will triumph in the end. It offers a powerful challenge to those whose christology begins with a human figure and devalues the divine nature. It presents as a mystery the supremacy of Christ over the events of history, but it comes to grips with the important aspect of consummation. A christology which does not include some vision of a New Jerusalem in which God and the Lamb are supreme, with all enemies defeated, must be regarded as inferior to that which constitutes the message of Revelation. Without this book in the canon the New Testament would be the poorer. As he faces its revelations John, the writer, responds in the only appropriate manner when he falls down in worship before the risen Christ (1:17).

The Church—Past, Present and Future

CHAPTER THREE

The Church—Past, Present and Future

There is certainly no doctrine of the church in the Apocalypse. But the book sheds a great deal of light not only on the condition of the church in the first century AD, but on the continuing state of the church in our modern age. While there are features which must be regarded as relevant only for the original readers, the underlying principles have an abiding significance. Our task will be not so much to examine in detail the exegesis of the more specifically ecclesiastical passages, but to present an overall impression of what can be deduced from the book as a whole in encouragement and warning for the modern church.

We shall begin with a statement of the relationship between the christology and the church, since this is of vital importance in our appreciation of the nature of the church. It is not without considerable importance that, in the structure of this book, the messages to the churches are prefaced by the vision in ch. 1, and that this vision provides (in most cases) the source for the various descriptions of the Person from whom the messages come. There is no doubt that the church has no independent existence outside a precise understanding of the status of Christ himself.

The Symbol of the Lampstands

The seven lampstands clearly bear some relation to the seven-branched lampstand of the tabernacle (Ex. 25:31ff) and of Zechariah's vision (ch. 4). But the fact that the one lampstand has now become seven is evidence of the freedom with which our author adapts his Old Testament models. It is not difficult to see why the seven-fold pattern was more useful for the author's purpose than the seven-branched form. He sees Christ in the midst and a seven-fold pattern could clearly be arranged in a circular manner in which the central figure is in equal proximity to each.

The imagery used here is suggestive for another reason. If the Christian church is seen as the medium through which light is brought to the world, in accordance with the teaching of Jesus (Mt. 5:14), the lampstand image is highly relevant. The command to shine as lights has never been revoked and must be regarded as a major objective for the communities of Christ to-day. It is all the more relevant in view of the increasing moral darkness which surrounds so much of modern life. It is significant that the claim of Jesus in one of John's 'I am' statements to be the Light of the world is thus developed in this vision of Christ in the midst of his churches. Any light they give is reflected light.

We note that the lampstands are described as golden, and this again has some symbolic significance. It is another feature drawn from Old

Testament sources. The reference to the most precious metal adds a sense of tremendous value to this representation of the churches. At the outset of the book the focus falls on the immense importance of the churches. Not only is the book addressed to specific churches, but its main thrust is intended to show God's estimate of his people.

The Symbol of the Stars

The seven stars seen in the right hand of Christ are a representation of the church, and present a further and somewhat different aspect from that implied by the lampstands. It is most likely that the language is indebted to Dn. 12:3: 'And those who are wise shall shine like the brightness of the firmament; and those who turn many to righteousness, like the stars for ever and ever'. Here the main significance lies not so much in the interpretation of the symbol as in the fact that the stars are grasped in the secure hand of Christ. Not only is Christ in the midst of his people, he is also their supporter. Here is an assurance that Christ has not left his church to their own devices, but has undertaken to protect and strengthen them.

This conception of the security of God's people is a key theme throughout the book. The cosmic drama which is unfolded is secondary to this. The basis of the message is that Christ is the protector of his people and at no time is the reader allowed to forget this. There is no question, even in the direct messages to the individual churches, of the earthly communities themselves being left to battle with the forces of darkness. While the churches are in the hand of Christ no harm can come to them. This affirmation is reinforced in the main body of the book in spite of the necessary calls to repentance in the letters of exhortation.

But a problem arises from the fact that the stars are identified in 1:20 as the angels of the churches, if the word *angeloi* is indeed intended to bear this sense. The problem may be thought to disappear if the alternative understanding of *angeloi* as messengers is preferred, since the stars would be identified with the church leaders.[1] Nevertheless it must not be supposed that the messages are addressed only to the leaders, for it is clear from the contents that they were intended for the whole church.[2] Yet it is undeniable that the messages to the churches are addressed to those who are securely held in the hands of Christ.[3] The impact of this initial vision is that the church is Christ-centred in every way.

The Seven Messages

The naming of the seven Asian churches is a potent reminder that this book must be interpreted in a historical context. There were churches at the cities mentioned. In many cases the allusions in

---

1. Whereas the interpretation of *angeloi* as messengers has support from O.T. usage, and could therefore be a reference to the leaders of the churches, it has the major disadvantage that elsewhere in this book John uses the word to describe heavenly beings.

2. Some see the background here of angels assigned to nations as in Daniel. G. R. Beasley-Murray, *Revelation* 69, uses this evidence to maintain that the angels are heavenly counterparts of the earthly communities.

3. Beasley-Murray, *idem* 70, discusses the pagan belief that the seven planets were symbolic of political power over the world, and suggests that John has chosen this as a way of affirming that Christ, not Caesar, holds the supreme power through his angels, which themselves represent the churches.

the individual messages have some bearing on the geographical and sociological environment of the cities concerned. These were the churches for whom the book was originally written. In our search for modern relevance we shall neglect at our peril this historical orientation. The historical basis indeed gives confidence in finding modern historical parallels.

Some comment should first be made about those theories which see in the messages a representation of the whole history of the church in its successive stages. If this type of theory were valid, our search for relevance would then be restricted to the message to the Laodicean church on the assumption that our present age is the last of the whole sequence. But this theory begs many questions. It depends not so much on exegesis as eisegesis, in that a seven-age scheme of church history must necessarily be forced on the text. It does not meet the criterion that the original readers must be expected to have understood the message, which on this view they clearly would have had no means of doing. We may dismiss this type of theory because of its basically non-historical approach.

But this leaves us with the need to look carefully at all the messages to discover their abiding contribution. The fact that all the letters have a similar structure points to a formalized construction. Although they are usually described as letters, that is an inaccurate description of them.[4] There is no way in which it can be

---

4. Beasley-Murray, *Revelation*, 72, refers to the view that they read more like oracles than letters, and cites Lohse's view of parallels with Amos chs. 1 and 2 (*Die Offenbarung des Johannes*, Göttingen, 1960).

maintained that each message is intended only for the church specifically addressed, since the whole book is intended for all the churches. They are still in view in ch. 22:16. In the light of this it is clear all the churches were intended to read all the messages, and each must be interpreted accordingly. We may legitimately take the main themes of these letters as being relevant to a wider context and apply them in a general sense as well as noting their immediate historical application.[5]

Ephesus

This church is given pride of place because of its influential position. Although Pergamum was the official capital, Ephesus was much larger, was on the main trade route, was a free city (i.e. a self-governing city), was the centre for the worship of Artemis and was notorious as a city of pagan superstition and immorality.[6] It was a tough place for the planting of the gospel and the message

---

5. Space will not allow a discussion of the view that the letters were originally distinct from the main body of the book. This has been held in two forms. R. H. Charles (*Revelation*, I xciv, 43–46) maintained they had been published several years before they were incorporated into the book. M. Goguel (*L'Eglise primitive*, 1947, Paris, 66) also placed them before the main body of the work, but for different reasons. He thought the approach to persecution was different. Yet others have come to the opposite conclusion from the same evidence and dated the letters later. Cf. M. Dibelius, 'Rom und die Christen im ersten Jahrhundert', *Botschaft und Geschichte* 2, 1956, 224. Some scholars have seen a close connection between the letters to the churches and the rest of the book. Cf. C. H. Parez, 'The Seven Letters and the Rest of the Apocalypse', *JTS* 12, 1911, 384–386. P. Minear, *I saw a New Earth—an Introduction to the Visions of the Apocalypse*, Washington 1968, finds parallels with the New Jerusalem passage. Cf. C. Hemer, *The Letters to the Seven Churches of Asia in their local setting*, Sheffield, 1986.

6. Cf. F. Miltner, *Ephesus, Stadt der Artemis und des Johannes*, Vienna 1958.

addressed to it must be viewed against this background. We may summarize the message to this church under two main themes—an assessment of their state and their approach to false teaching. Under the first theme, we note their positive achievements. They had toiled and exerted themselves greatly in the cause of the gospel. They had not slackened in the work. For a church set in so adverse an environment, it is high commendation that they had persevered in spite of the odds. They had moreover shown considerable discernment in that they had recognized the dubious character of some who were claiming apostolic status. This combination of hard work and insight is formidable.

Their approach to false teaching is also highly commended. They hate the Nicolaitans,[7] who are linked in 2:15 with those who hold the teaching of Balaam. It may be significant that the Greek root behind 'Nicolaus' and the Hebrew root behind 'Balaam' possibly both mean 'to conquer the people'. Certainly Balaam, according to Numbers 25:1–5, seduced the people and caused them to sin. According to the message to Pergamum the false teaching was connected with meat offered to idols and with immorality. It was clearly a threat to the Christian faith. At a time when the church was in its infancy it was of utmost importance that true worship and true morals should be jealously guarded, and both were under attack. It says much for the young Ephesian church that they were alert enough and discerning enough to

---

7. On Gnostic parallels providing a possible explanation of the Nicolaitans, cf. E. S. Fiorenza, 'Apocalyptic and Gnosis in the Book of Revelation', *JBL* 92, 1973, 565–581. Cf also W. M. Mackay, 'Another Look at the Nicolaitans', *EQ* 45, 1973, 111–115, who finds evidence of syncretism.

recognize the threat and to hate it. It poses a challenge for the modern church to discover to what extent its own attempts to preserve purity of doctrine and of practice would be commended by the Lord of the church. The permissive society has invaded the church to such an extent that loose morals are sometimes tolerated in a way which would not have happened in Ephesus.

Yet there is an important ground for criticism. The Christians of Ephesus have lost their first love. We need to determine the nature of the love, and two interpetations are possible. They have either lost their first love for Christ, or they have lost their first love for each other. Both, of course, may be in mind, but it is most likely that the latter is intended. Perhaps the penetrating insight which enabled them to hate the false teaching led to a harsh attitude towards those affected by that teaching. It is not unknown for enthusiasts for truth to be lacking in generosity, when the flame of orthodoxy has tended to overwhelm the fires of love. But this result is undesirable and need not be. Those who rightly crusade for truth should be on their guard against the danger that love for the brethren will be eroded.

So great is this possibility that the Risen Lord issues three commands—'remember . . .', 'repent . . .' and 'do . . .'. Repentance is a recurring call in these letters, but in none is the cause (lack of love) so unexpected.

Smyrna

The church in Smyrna was in a city generally recognized to have been the most beautiful in Asia. It had many pagan temples and was at the time prosperous and influential. It had been intensely loyal to Rome and as a reward it had been declared a free city. In its earlier history it had experienced a kind of resurrection, when the new city was founded in c. 290 BC.[8]

The most outstanding feature about the church is that it had been subjected to intense opposition from the Jews. It is known that the Jewish population of the city was both large and influential, and it is not surprising that persecution of the Christian church developed there. The Risen Christ calls the opposition 'the synagogue of Satan', a devastating judgment on those who imagined they were serving God in opposing the church. An important assurance in this letter is the limited period of the persecution. The 'ten days' is a short and strictly circumscribed period showing that the persecutors are not in control.

What stood out in this church was its poverty. In an environment of wealth this was particularly noticeable. The probable reason was that the majority of the believers were drawn from the lower classes, although some may have become poor as a consequence of the adverse action of their persecutors. History has repeated itself many times in this respect, but in our affluent Western society the situation has tended to be reversed. It is often more difficult to reach the poorer people with the gospel than the more affluent middle classes. The main lesson in the message to this church is that there is no correlation between material prosperity and spiritual riches, for the Lord pronounces these poverty-stricken believers to be rich. This assertion of their spiritual superiority is borne out by the absence of any command to repent, a feature shared only by the church at Philadelphia. The

8. Cf. C. J. Cadoux, *Ancient Smyrna*, Oxford 1938.

relevance of this new standard of values for our modern age needs no underlining.

Pergamum

In 133 BC the province of Asia was established as part of the Roman Empire, with Pergamum as its capital. Prior to that it had been the capital of the Seleucid Kingdom.[9] In spite of the fact that it was not so well situated on the trade routes as Ephesus or Smyrna, it nevertheless exercised considerable political influence. It was impressively situated at the top of a rocky hill. It was famous for its remarkable library, which contained more than 200,000 parchment scrolls, and was second only to that of Alexandria. It was in fact the place where parchment was first used instead of papyri.

But in addition to being a place of culture, Pergamum was notorious for the shrine to Zeus which stood in a prominent position on the top of its rocky pinnacle. This may have prompted the reference to 'Satan's throne', or the reference may have been to the Temple of Asclepios, whose emblem was a serpent. The latter, however, was a shrine of healing, and it is difficult to think that it would call forth the description of Satan's seat. Another possibility is that the city itself, as the official seat of the proconsul and the administrative centre for emperor worship, was seen as Satan's seat because Christians were being persecuted there if they refused to call Caesar Lord.

Corroborative evidence supporting the theory that 'Satan's seat' refers to emperor worship may be present in the description of the Risen Christ as having a double-edged sword, since the proconsul would have had the right to such a sword (*ius*

9. Cf. E. V. Hansen, *The Attilids of Pergamon*, New York 1947.

gladii). In this way the Christians were assured that the ultimate sovereignty did not rest with Rome. They had nevertheless remained loyal to Christ. The clash between the worship of God and the worship of the state is a recurring problem and no less crucial in our modern times. The clash of ideologies, particularly in the communist world, has led to the imprisonment of many and many an 'Antipas' has been put to death. The experience of the Pergamum church could not be more relevant. Moreover it is worthy of note that the church was living and witnessing in the very city where Satan is said to live, reminding us that the most powerful witness is often in places where opposition is most intense.

Yet again, here at Pergamum, we meet with problems within the fellowship. The Nicolaitans are as active here as in Ephesus, but the church has not been so discerning as to hate them. Indeed, repentance is needed here, a recognition that the false teaching is dangerous. The sword from the mouth of the risen Christ is strongly opposed to the false teachings. The message to the Pergamum church contains an implicit warning that not all churches are equally equipped to detect and deal with aberrations of teaching and particularly of behaviour.

Thyatira
This city lay on the road from Pergamum to Sardis. It was a less important town but was nevertheless a centre for commerce. Lydia, the cloth trader mentioned in Acts 16:14, came from this city. It was also a city of many guilds. It may be that these guilds were a problem for the Christians, for the feasts associated with them were dominated by pagan ideas which made it difficult

for Christians to be guild members. The temptation to compromise would be great, but the warning against doing so is strong.

The Jezebel movement seems to have been a part of the general false teachings which have already been encountered in Ephesus and Pergamum. Why mention is made of Jezebel is not clear, but she was presumably the leader of the movement.[10] There was a shrine at Thyatira at which a female oracle named Sambathe presided and 'Jezebel' might be a veiled allusion to this. The features singled out are immorality and idolatry. The church is criticized for tolerating this woman. They were evidently taking a lenient line. The command to repent of this is strong and the dangers which would be incurred through not doing so are stringent. Nevertheless many of the Christians had not fallen prey to her and had not learned Satan's secrets. This latter term would seem to imply some esoteric counterfeit knowledge diametrically opposed to Christian truth. Again purity of teaching and of practice are seen to be vital for the emerging church.

If at this early stage in Christian history such inroads had been made, it is incumbent on the churches in each succeeding age to examine their approach to wrong teaching. Is the modern church vigilant enough? Has it become too permissive towards those who deviate from the purity of doctrine and high moral demands of New Testament Christianity?

Sardis
Here was a place which had a glorious past, but its

---

10. Cf. E. Schürer, 'Die Prophetin Isabel in Thyatira', *TLZ* 18, 1893, 153–154.

splendour had gone. It had had a reputation for wealth, particularly in the time of the legendary Croesus. Yet it was that king who had been responsible for the collapse of the kingdom. Although Sardis was situated on an apparently impregnable rock, twice in its history (in 546 BC and in 214 BC), it had fallen to invaders because of the friable character of the rock which enabled footholds to be gained in it. The exhortation to vigilance and the need for strengthening may well be an allusion to these historic facts. So also is the reference to coming as a thief, which aptly describes the way in which the city had been attacked in former years. It is noteworthy also that the city was well known as a centre for the woollen industry and this may be reflected in the allusion to unsoiled garments.[11]

The Christian church in this city is criticized because it did not live up to its reputation as a living church. It was in fact dead—a devastating judgment. This spiritual deadness had produced an enervating effect on the usefulness of the church. It was as well that no false teaching troubled them, for they seem to have been too apathetic to bother about heresy. The strong message to these people is a challenge to wake up. Clearly the deadness is not so far gone that it is useless to issue such a challenge to them. They are still in a position to do something about it; they are told to remember, to obey and repent.

Sardis is representative of church life which has become inactive. A church like this can be ignored. It is not even worthwhile for false teachers to attack it. If it ceased to function this

11. Cf. D. Mitten, 'A New Look at Ancient Sardis', *BA* 29, 1966, 38–68.

would make little difference. Yet there was one bright spot in Sardis. A minority had not soiled their clothes, which presumably means they were unaffected by the surrounding deadness, or it may imply freedom from the immorality which was a feature of their environment. The message here is highly relevant. We must not write off whole churches as ineffective, since there is always the possibility that some faithful people remain who will redeem the situation. What is most striking is the purity of these people. It is not their capabilities, or their understanding of Christian truth, but their moral behaviour. Such people can be a spiritual force even in an otherwise dead church.

The dressing of these people in white is symbolic. The elders in the heavenly scene in ch. 4 are dressed in white, as are the multitude of worshippers in ch. 7, and the armies which came from heaven in ch. 19. Moreover, the souls of the martyrs in ch. 6 are each given a white robe and told to wait for God to act. The white dress is therefore symbolic of the true worshippers of God. Whiteness is in any case an apt description of purity. This fits in with the early Christian practice of giving people who had just been baptized a clean white robe. The active Christian life is essentially a life with high standards of purity. There may also be some allusion to the white toga worn by Romans at festival times.

The idea of these people walking with the risen Christ arrayed in their white robes may derive something from a pagan background, as for instance the privileges granted by Persian kings to their favoured companions to walk with them in the royal gardens. The promise to the overcoming Christian is of a permanent walk with the risen Christ. The right to do so will be demonstrated by the white dress, which is not merely formal dress, but symbolic of worthiness.

Philadelphia

The situation of this city was strategic for the dissemination of ideas. Founded comparatively recently, it had been most effective for spreading the language and literature of Greece in Lydia and Phrygia. It was therefore an admirable place for the spread of the gospel and this fact may well be the explanation of the open door mentioned in the letter. As with so many other of the surrounding cities it was affected by the earthquake of AD 17, but it was also plagued by a continuous series of tremors for some time afterwards. Most of the inhabitants had fled from the city and erected temporary accommodation outside the walls. Philadelphia was so grateful to Tiberius for his help in rebuilding the city that the name was changed to Neocaesarea and yet again to Flavia in the time of Vespasian. The idea of receiving a new name was therefore familiar to the people of this city.

The church here is commended, without any exhortation to repent. Although it is clearly restricted in strength, yet an open door has been set before it. Its lack of strength is not criticized because its members have not denied the name of Christ. Faithfulness is more important than power, a salutary reminder to the church of all ages, not least to our own.

There are apparently no problems here, but a promise is included which has a bearing on the relationship between the Christian community and the Jews. The risen Christ assures the Christians that Jews, who are described as the synagogue of Satan, will come to acknowledge that Christ has loved his church. Presumably the reference to Satan implies that the Jews in question are those who have specifically done Satan's work in opposing and obstructing the Christian church. Those who had experienced such opposition would find encouragement in this promise. As far as its modern relevance is concerned, the condemnation of this letter may be extended to include all those who wrongly claim to be the people of God.

Perhaps in the background to this letter there is the Jewish belief in the two ages which would be separated by a time of destruction. This may account for the allusion to the time of trial, although it must be remembered that in all probability the Christians regarded the age to come as already arrived in Christ. The time of trial is more likely to refer to the persecution which seems to loom on the horizon throughout this book. It is clearly of some intensity since it will affect the whole world. If the phrase refers to the final judgment, it is intended to reassure the Christians of deliverance at that time.

The command given to this church is of universal relevance. 'Hold on to what you have' may not seem progressive enough for many in our modern society, but progress in spiritual matters is not gained by jettisonning the basis of the faith. In no age can the church afford to neglect the foundations on which it is built. The advice to hold on is not reactionary conservatism, but an indispensable challenge.

The promise that the overcomer will be made a pillar in God's temple may be an allusion to the practice of erecting pillars in temples to celebrate the long service of faithful priests. Instead of bearing the name of an individual, however, this pillar is inscribed with the name of God, of the

New Jerusalem and of Christ. There would be no doubt to whom he belonged. The assurance that he would not leave the temple might well be of significance to those who were having to leave their homes in Philadelphia through the earth tremors, another case of the local colour being used to good effect. But the general assurance of the security of God's people has timeless significance.

Laodicea

Here was a church in a wealthy and distinguished city. Laodicea was situated on the main road from Ephesus to Syria and was the crossing point of other important roads. It is small wonder that it became a place of wealth. It was renowned for three things, all of which influenced the language used to describe the spiritual condition of the church.

There were many financial houses in Laodicea which made it one of the foremost banking centres of the world. So wealthy was it that the citizens were able to rebuild the city after the earthquake of AD 61 without the aid of the government. But wealth which bred such self-sufficiency so invaded the church that it did not recognize its spiritual poverty, a state of affairs which has many times been repeated in the history of the Christian church.

Laodicea was also the centre for a widely known type of black clothing, made from the wool of the local breed of sheep. The spiritual nakedness of the Laodicean church was in vivid contrast to their pride in their garments. Similarly, although the city was also famous for its medical school and the production of ointment for ears and eyes, it was blissfully unaware of its own spiritual blindness.

In none of the letters to the Asian churches is the local colour so vividly used as here. The church in this centre was clearly affected by its environment. We may say that the relevance of this message is experienced in any situation in which self-sufficiency is the main characteristic of the church. Wherever this applies there is nothing but condemnation from the Lord of the church. Never is this more potent than when a Christian community exists in an affluent society and allows itself to be governed by the conventions and moral code of its environment.

The condemnation of this church is expressed in terms even more vivid than we find in the other messages. The great strategic weakness of Laodicea was its reliance on an extensive conduit for its water supply. Between its source in the hot springs of Hierapolis and its terminus in Laodicea it absorbed lime and became tepid.[12] The water was not palatable. The natural reaction was to spit it out. Everyone in the city would know this, but the Christians must have been shocked to discover that Christ expressed his view of them in the very same terms. Their own self-image is expressed in a statement of nauseating smugness —'I have need of nothing.'

The advice given is devasting, yet in some sense reassuring. They are to 'buy' from Christ gold, clothes and eye ointment, the very things they thought they could depend on obtaining from the city. But what Christ offers is of a different kind. The gold is purified, not soiled; the garments are white, not black; the eye ointment is for their spiritual sight, not for their physical eyes. It

---

12. Cf. M. J. S. Rudwick and E. M. B. Green, 'The Laodicean Lukewarmness', *ET* 69, 1957, 8, 176–178.

is deeply humiliating. The complacency which seemed so soundly based is shattered. The church is back to square one. Yet it is not wiped off altogether. There is time to repent. Christ may be outside the door, but he is still there and knocking. It is amazing that even such Christians receive an invitation to enjoy a fellowship meal with the risen Christ. The situation, appalling as it is, is not beyond remedy.

Perhaps the most disturbing message for the modern church is that the greatest concern expressed does not relate to heresy, important as that is, but to complacency and self-sufficiency. Even the orthodox can reach the stage of saying, 'I have need of nothing'. There has probably never been a time in Christian history when this message has been more needed, especially in an affluent society. It is easy to lose sight of the fact that spiritual wealth is of much greater value in the sight of God than material resources. It could perhaps be said that the Laodicean church is a prime example of harmful interaction between a Christian community and its environment.

The Church at Worship

The Book of Revelation contains many liturgical sections. It may be questioned to what extent the hymns reflect fragments of existing worship or are to be regarded as in some sense patterns for such worship. Even if we should conclude that the hymns must be regarded as heavenly liturgies having no connection with the historical procedures of the contemporary church, we may still find some relevance in these hymns as indications of worship patterns worth following.

Various proposals have been made interpreting the liturgical material as having been incorporated into the book from earlier sources. If it could be established that this had happened, it would furnish valuable evidence of the kind of worship followed by the Christian communities to which the book was written. One theory is that such traces of earlier material can be detected from a study of the doxologies, the acclamations of worthiness, the Trisagion in 4:8, and examples of hymnic material which is not in agreement with its context. This approach has been advocated by J. O'Rourke,[13] who has argued that the evidence shows that the material is not the author's own creation. But his contentions have been challenged on the grounds that the parallels he brings forward are inconclusive. For instance when he says that the doxology in 7:12 would not have been out of place in a Jewish liturgy, he is using a method of argument that adds nothing to the debate.

Another writer, A. B. Macdonald,[14] distinguishes between some of the hymns as being Christian (5:9–14; 12:10–12; 19:1ff and 19:5–8) and some as derived from the Greek-speaking synagogue (4:11; 15:3ff; 11:15–18 and 7:12). A modification of the same view is advocated by R. P. Martin.[15] It has however been strongly argued that the linguistic evidence on which these theories are based is insufficient to establish dependence on Hellenistic sources.[16]

---

13. 'The Hymns of the Apocalypse', *CBQ* 30, 1968, 399–409.
14. *Christian Worship in the Primitive Church,* Edinburgh 1934, 112ff.
15. *Worship on the Early Church,* London 1964, 45.
16. R. Deichgräber, *Gotteshymnus und Christushymnus: Untersuchungen zu Form, Sprach und Stil der frühchristlichen Hymnen,* Göttingen 1967, 52, considered that both Christian and Jewish

Various other theories have supposed that the hymnic material in this book goes back to an existing liturgical sequence. These theories have taken different forms. Some appeal to eucharistic practice, seeing in the hymns the influence either of Johannine eucharistic usage[17] or of a liturgy localized in Asia Minor.[18] The former theory rests on an appeal to 1 Clement and the Didache, but it is strongly disputed whether this evidence has anything to do with the liturgy.[19] The latter theory is somewhat speculative and appeals to mid-second century practice, which is not convincing. Equally unproven is the view that the details of worship in Revelation are connected with the Sunday eucharist pattern described by Justin.[20]

Another suggestion is that the Christians at an early date adapted a synagogue liturgy for use in Christian worship. It has been proposed that chapters 4 and 5 can be reconstructed in the form of a liturgy as follows: Invitation, Trisagion, Praise to God as Creator, Prostration by the congregation, Reading of Scripture, Prayer with praise to Christ as the slain Lamb, ending with the Doxology and choral Amen.[21] This is suggestive,

---

elements are to be found in most of the hymns. Cf. also O. Cullmann, *Early Christian Worship,* London 1953, 21, and M. Dibelius, *A Fresh Approach to the New Testament and Early Christian Literature,* London 1936, 247. Cf. also R. Bauckham, 'The worship of Jesus in Apocalyptic Christianity', *NTS* 27, 1980–81, 322–341.

17. D. M. Stanley, 'Carmenque Christo quasi Deo dicere . . .' *CBQ* 20, 1958, 182–183.

18. S. Läuchli, 'Eine Gottesdienststruktur in der Johannesoffenbarung', *ThZ* 16, 1960, 359–378.

19. Cf. W. C. van Unnik, 'I Clement 34 and the Sanctus', *Vigiliae Christianae* 5, 1951, 204–208.

20. So A. Cabaniss, 'A Note on the Liturgy of the Apocalypse', *Interpretation* 7, 1953, 78–80.

21. L. Mowry, 'Rev. 4–5 and Early Christian Liturgical Usage', *JBL* 71, 1952, 75–84.

but involves treating the elders as representatives of the congregation. Nevertheless, it is possible to see a symbolic pattern of acceptable worship in the heavenly scene without supposing that it was derived from synagogue sources. Attempts to find a liturgy behind this book have been persistent, but it may be that too much has been supposed about early Christian worship without adequate support. There is undoubtedly a gap in our knowledge of early Christian liturgies which makes it difficult to be certain.

It has often been argued that the hymnic material in this book was composed by the author himself, in which case the question of the liturgy remains open. The accounts of heavenly worship may have been suggested by forms of worship currently in use, but the evidence does not require this. The problem arises as to why the writer should have transferred the worship to a heavenly scene if the suggestions have come from an earthly counterpart. It is profitable to enquire what function the heavenly worship scenes serve in the purpose of the whole book before we conclude that the passages have been influenced by contemporary worship. If the passages concerned are a vital key to the appreciation of the apocalypse as a whole, which seems undeniable, we should not wrest them from their context without taking into account their essentially eschatological purpose. The liturgical passages are not an end in themselves but lead up to the great crescendo in chapters 21 and 22.

We may summarize some of the lessons the hymns convey in order to show their present relevance, before passing on to consider the significance of the New Jerusalem. Worship must certainly be based on a high view of God. Here he is presented as so exalted that he can be alluded to as the one on the throne without even being named (4:2; 7:10). He is adored as holy and almighty (4:8; 15:4). He is seen as Creator and thus perceived as glorious and powerful in his creation (4:11). He is associated with the Lamb as the most worthy object of worship (5:13; 21:22). In his presence the four living creatures and the elders fall down in dignified adoration. His power is unquestioned and his reign has begun (11:17,18). His ways are just and true (15:3,4; 19:2). Through his Son God is the redeemer of mankind (5:9; 19:1).

It is significant that these worship passages are completely devoid of introspection on the part of the worshippers. Exclusive attention is given to the character and acts of God, which so dominate the scene that worship is spontaneous. The relevance of this fact for modern worship is not far to seek. Spontaneity in worship is one of the outstanding features of modern progressive Christianity. In a remarkable way the body of Christ is learning to pour out praise to the One who is worthy to receive it. This is a healthier approach than to spend time bemoaning the weakness and impotence of the church. The God who is worshipped in Revelation is a glorious God whose strength and power are seen when he acts on behalf of his people.

But the climax of the book is in chs. 21 and 22, for which the worship scenes have progressively prepared us.[22] The New Jerusalem visions are

---

22. L. Thompson, 'Cult and Eschatology in the Apocalypse of John', *Journal of Religion* 49, 1969, 330–350, points out that the heavenly worship ceases before the account of the New Jerusalem, because it has no further preparatory purpose. It must be noted that K-P Jörns, *Das hymnische Evangelium,* although he recognized that the hymns form the connecting link between the visions, did not bring out the link between them and the final vision of the New Jerusalem.

highly relevant for the church on earth, for they paint a picture of the future. They bring hope to the struggling earthly communities. They present a glorious consummation. The church has previously been described as a bride totally ready and suitably dressed for the marriage supper of the Lamb. Whatever the weaknesses reflected in the opening letters, a time dawns when the church is arrayed in fine linen, bright and pure (19:8). After the coming of the warrior King, as the Lamb is now pictured, the New Jerusalem descends. God declares that everything is being made new. Yet how relevant is the new Jerusalem for the modern Christian? The vision has often been dismissed as 'pie-in-the-sky', intended to distract the readers from thinking about their present problems? But this is not how the book of Revelation portrays it. Here it is natural consummation of God's plan of salvation.

The city image is significant. It symbolizes redeemed man in community. It is no ordinary city. Its cubelike dimensions are clearly symbolic. It is highly relevant to remember that the central feature of Old Testament worship is a cube, the Holy of Holies, but whereas only one man was eligible once a year to enter there, now the whole community is placed within the cube. The eschatological significance is unavoidable. At the last, in spite of the problems arising from the conflict with evil, God's plans work out triumphantly in the perfection of his people. All the details of the New Jerusalem are intended to point to that perfection —the jewels, the gates, the light from God and the Lamb, the pure gold of the city and the river of life. Sorrow and death are banished for ever. Those who work evil are excluded. Nothing remains to mar the bliss of the people of God. No greater comfort could be given to Christians today, so often faced with intense challenge, than a vision of the New Jerusalem. There is no more triumphant book than this in the New Testament; here the modern church can find fresh courage.

Conclusion

As we have examined the various aspects of the church in this book we have seen that in many ways Revelation has great relevance for the modern church. Even in the first century the condition of the church was far from uniform and the varied messages provide us to-day with a selection of situations which are reminiscent of many features of modern church life.

Christians to-day need the assurance of Christ's presence in the midst as much as the first century church. We cannot regard the Christian community as a product of man's ingenuity. It is of the nature of New Testament Christianity that the church cannot be rightly perceived apart from a right understanding of the person of Christ. Today the risen Christ still sustains his people by his powerful right hand.

As for the worship passages although they do not provide us with a liturgy, yet they certainly supply us with much inspiration to worship. The repeated adulation of God and of the Lamb constitute a picture of worship which has much to challenge and inspire Christians of the twentieth century.

The Conflict and its Consummation

CHAPTER FOUR

The Conflict and its Consummation

Our last major study will focus on the idea of combat in Revelation. Even a cursory reading must impress on the reader's mind that there is conflict not only in the earthly realm, but in the heavenly. Spiritual forces are locked in combat and yet the outcome is never in doubt. As we examine the features of this conflict we shall discover what message this aspect of the book has for the modern world. We shall begin by noting the forces arrayed against God and his people. We shall then examine the various symbols used to express the nature of the opposition. In order to put this in perspective we shall need to enquire into the background of the combat idea. We shall conclude with comments on judgment and consummation in Revelation, before relating the whole imagery to the modern scene.

Evidences of Conflict against God

John is in exile on Patmos (1:9)
Probably Patmos was a penal settlement. John

95

states that he was there on account of the word of God and the testimony of Jesus. This points to a situation in which a clash had occurred between Christians and the authorities. It is not necessary to suppose that a general period of persecution had broken out, but certainly in some way John had fallen foul of the state for him to be exiled on this island. But this was a blessing in disguise for him since it put him in the frame of mind to receive these visions.

Smyrna will know persecution (2:10)
In the message to Smyrna it is stated that the devil was about to cast some members of the church into prison. In his message to the church Christ regards this as a time of testing. It is strictly limited, as the mention of ten days makes clear.[1] There is no need to attach any precise meaning to the ten days other than a specified and short period. The implication is that there are definite restrictions on the devil's activities—unless the meaning is that the believers' destiny for life or death will be soon decided.[2] At this early stage in the book we are not allowed to forget that it is written against a background of opposition and persecution.

Antipas has died in Pergamum (2:13)
The death of Antipas had happened in the city which is described as containing Satan's throne. As we have seen (page 00) this is most likely a reference to the fact that Pergamum was a centre

---

1. J. M. Court, *Myth and History*, 30, thinks this may be an allusion to the Niobe tradition in Homer's *Iliad*, 24.602–617, where the tenth day terminates the period of mourning, on the grounds that the Niobe tradition had local significance.
2. So Beasley-Murray, *Revelation, ad. loc.*

for emperor worship. Two other explanations have been put forward. It has been pointed out that the city was also a centre for the worship of Asclepios, whose symbol was a serpent. Since there was also there an enormous altar to Zeus on the acropolis, it has been suggested that this might have given rise to the idea of Satan's throne. But it is most likely that the existence of the emperor worship centre provides the best explanation. We hear nothing more of Antipas, who is the only named witness in this book to die for the faith.[3] It appears that opposition to the gospel in Pergamum was more intense than it had yet been in Smyrna.

Philadelphia is reminded of the hour of trial (3:10)
The trial appears to affect the whole of mankind and is not here a testing of Christians. Some take it to refer to the messianic woes which are later mentioned, and this seems most likely. Unlike the Smyrnaean situation, it is God not the devil who inaugurates the testing. This will explain why the people of God are promised protection.[4] The testing is of those who have aligned themselves against him.

The martyrs cry for vengeance under the altar (6:9–11)
The idea of God avenging his people after a set time occurs in 1 Enoch 47, where the holy ones unite in prayer to him.[5] Jesus predicted that his

---

3. R. H. Charles, *Revelation, ad. loc.,* regarded the word *martus* here as meaning martyr, but it is more likely that it was intended in the sense of witness.
4. This trial may possibly be seen in the context of the continuous 'trial' of the Philadelphians, constantly living under the threat of earthquake tremors.
5. Beasley-Murray, *Revelation, ad loc.,* gives the citation in full because of its significance.

people would suffer persecution (Mk. 13:9ff. cf. Mt. 23:29ff). It is generally supposed that 'under the altar' means in the presence of God. The cry for vengeance makes poignant the plight of the Christians in an alien environment.[6] It is a situation with which the readers would be able readily to identify. Perhaps the testimony of these people had been misrepresented as an undermining of the state, and the Christians wanted the record put straight. They are assured that God would act, but are warned of the need for patience.[7]

A triumphant throng come out of the great tribulation (7:14)

This looks back from the end time to the tribulation which preceded the parousia (cf. 3:10). The use of the article denotes the whole series of calamities, not any one specifically. It sums up in a word the entire sequence of harassments to the Christian church which would occur before the coming of Christ. The great throng in white robes and carrying palm branches cries out that salvation is from God and the Lamb (verse 10). God's people have survived the tribulation, but they have not escaped it. They have experienced the protection of God (verse 15) and now receive a promise that their sorrows are over. This conception of the great tribulation focuses on the central conflict portrayed in this book. It is not the kind of tribulation which happens through circumstances, but results from a deliberate attack on God's people whipped up by

---

6. G. Caird, *Revelation,* 84, considers that these martyrs were among those who were killed in the Neronian persecution.

7. It should be noted that the cry of the martyrs, 'How long?' is probably indebted to Zech. 1:12, although applied in a different way. Zech. 1:13 contains words of consolation from God.

satanic agencies, as the visions of the book proceed to make clear.

The two witnesses are killed by the beast (11:7)
Two witnesses appear on the scene and are granted power to prophesy for a period of three and a half years (11:3). There is dispute over the nature of their testimony.[8] The fact that it is accompanied by great power is more in line with prophetic announcements, which characteristically include signs, than with the preaching of the gospel. Yet whatever the content of their message, it is a message from God. They are representatives of God and the Beast is totally and unremittingly opposed to them. Although the Beast conquers them and kills them, he does not win, for God breathes new life into them. This is a vivid reminder to the hard-pressed readers of the hollowness of whatever victory the Beast appears to gain. It must be noted that the rejoicing of 'the dwellers on the earth' clearly allies them with the Beast, and therefore identifies them as antagonists of God.

The male child is threatened (12:4)
The intention of the dragon to devour the child shows his implacable hatred towards Christ, who is undoubtedly represented by the male child. The allusion to Ps. 2:9 (LXX) makes this clear. The dragon can rightly be regarded as antichrist, although the term is not used in this book to describe him. The removal of the child suggests a defeat for the dragon. His casting out is reminiscent of the statement in Jn. 12:31: 'Now is the judgement of this world, now shall the ruler of this

---

8. Cf. the detailed discussion about these witnesses in J. M. Court, *Myth and history*, 82–105.

world be cast out'. In its original context, this statement is made in anticipation of the passion of Jesus and must be connected with it. Because of the cross the devil is already seen as a defeated foe. The worst he could do in the life of Jesus was to tempt him. The Gospels nowhere suggest that the cross itself was initiated by the devil to thwart God's plan, although the betrayal by Judas is attributed to him. There is constant tension in the New Testament between this divine plan and the design of the devil. The view that God was taken unawares when Jesus was crucified finds no support in the New Testament. Although wicked men performed the act, it was according to God's plan, as Peter made clear in his first sermon (Acts 2:23). In Rev. 12 the catching up of the male child evidently represents the life-death-resurrection-ascension of Christ considered as one event.[9]

The woman flees from the dragon (12:6,13f)
The switch from antagonism against Christ to antagonism against the people of God is the real key to this passage (see verse 17). The fact that the woman flees to the wilderness may be compared with the experience of the Israelites in the wilderness. Again there is a restriction on the time which is allowed for this antagonism to vent itself against God's people. It is limited to three and a half years. This probably refers to an intense time of opposition before the parousia. The conflict-theme is vividly portrayed in terms of the

---

9. For a detailed examination of the various theories concerning this chapter, cf. P. Prigent, *Apocalypse 12. Histoire de l'exégése*, Tübingen 1959. Prigent himself, while conceding Old Testament influences, favours the view that behind the dragon is the idea of temporal powers opposed to the Messiah, as for instance Herod at his birth.

serpent pouring water out of his mouth to drown the woman and the earth swallowing the water to protect her. There is special mention here of the anger of the dragon. As an intensification of this anger, two other beasts appear, both represented as agents of the dragon. It is not without significance that at this point a triumvirate or trinity of evil emerges as the conflict intensifies. Throughout the book evil counterfeits the good in an effort to gain its end.

Michael and his angels fight the dragon (12:7ff)
It is possible that this is a 'flashback' to the fall of Satan, referred to by Jesus in Lk. 10:18, this reference being itself an allusion to Isaiah 14:12. But it may reflect the current belief that Michael, as the heavenly champion against the devil, must expel Satan from heaven before Messiah can reign. If it had been intended as a flashback, it would have reminded the readers that the dragon's power is severely circumscribed. Whatever the explanation, the main thrust of the passage is to show that Satan has no place in heaven and has been effectively cast out.

The kings make war against the Lamb (17:14)
There has been much discussion over the identification of the kings in this chapter. Many exegetes have supposed that they represent the successive Roman emperors, but the precise identification is difficult. For our present purpose we may note that if they are representatives of the state, they are seen to be vassals of the Beast. Indeed, since they are described in terms of the horns of the Beast, the symbolism suggests that the secular authorities are dominated by evil agencies. Even if there is no connection here with the emperors as

such, the Kings certainly represent those who are in opposition to God. They are of one mind in making war against the Lamb. Since this episode is placed towards the conclusion of the book and is connected with the overthrow of Babylon, it focuses on the last phases of the conflict. The whole matter is expressed in terms of black and white. There are two sides only—the Beast and his minions confronting the Lamb and his armies.[10] But the outcome is not in doubt. The Lamb has already overcome.

The Lord of Lords fights against the beast and the kings (19:19)
If chapter 17 is descriptive of the opposing forces, chapter 19 gives the outcome of the clash. Powerful as the Beast may appear to be, his armies wilt before the triumphal appearance of the King of kings and Lord of lords. There is no description of any battle. The armies of heaven are arrayed for a wedding rather than for a war. The warrior King conquers not through military power, but through the sword proceeding from his mouth. His devastating command is enough. The account ends with a description of the vultures feasting on the carnage. In no more vivid way could the opposition of evil against God be expressed, nor the utter futility of the forces of darkness. Such affirmation would be of invaluabe worth to the original readers suffering under persecution.

Satan is released to deceive the nations (20:7,8)
This brief release is one of the most mysterious

---

10. R. H. Mounce, *The Book of Revelation,* Grand Rapids 1977, 318, points out that the idea of the righteous taking part in the destruction of the wicked is a standard apocalyptic theme.

episodes in a book which is full of mysteries. There appears to be some influence from the book of Ezekiel (38:1ff). The mention of Gog and Magog in this context certainly comes from the use of these names in Ezekiel. The Tell el-Amarna tablets use Gog as a name for the northern nations. The idea of the nations assaulting Israel is found in Jewish apocalyptic writings (2 Enoch 56:5ff; 2 Esdras 13:5ff; Sib. Or. 3:662ff). But although this explains the identification of the allies of Satan here, it does nothing to explain the loosing of Satan. There is no space to outline the many proposals towards a solution.[11] Suffice it to observe that in chapter 19 the kings of the earth are entirely destroyed and the Beast defeated, while chapter 20 is more concerned about the nations than the kings. Here Satan is allowed a final foray before being cast into the lake of fire. The conflict situation is permitted right up to the revelation of the great white throne.

We have seen how integral the conflict motif is to the whole book. We are not allowed to forget that the battle is constantly raging between spiritual forces. But we need to examine more closely the descriptions of the forces of evil in order to discover how far they are relevant for our present age.

---

11. Caird, *Revelation*, 256, thinks the release of Satan was dictated by John's belief that the millenium must be followed by a recrudescence of demonic evil. But this does not explain the reason for the release. G. E. Ladd, *Revelation*, Grand Rapids 1972, 269, suggests that the release after the millenium is intended to demonstrate that man's willingness to be seduced is not due to an adverse environment. M. Rissi, *The Future of the World,* London 1972, 26, points out that this last rebellion has only one purpose, i.e. to reveal Satan's powerlessness.

Symbols of Evil in Revelation

We have already seen that Satan is portrayed as
the arch-enemy of God in this book. We have
noted how the name occurs in the messages to the
seven churches. This general name of God's
adversary is used in conjunction with other
descriptions which reward careful study.

There are various designations of evil agencies
which are connected with the bottomless pit. In
one case the personification of evil is called the
angel of the pit (9:11) and his name is specified as
'Abaddon', which means 'destruction'. The Greek
equivalent is also given in the name Apollyon,
which some have supposed to be an allusion to the
god Apollo, but this seems unlikely. What is
beyond dispute is the destructive character of this
ruler of the pit. This in fact is a major feature of
the evil forces in this book. They are totally
negative, compared with the creative and redemptive forces initiated by God. In 11:7 this angel is
specifically described as the beast from the bottomless pit.

Other descriptions of Satan which are used in
this book are 'the great red dragon' (12:4), and 'the
ancient serpent' (12:9; 20:2). The latter term is
clearly derived from the Genesis story in which
the serpent beguiles the woman and thus gains the
name of 'deceiver of the whole world' (12:9). Jewish
readers would have no difficulty in recognizing
the source of this imagery, and even Gentiles who
had taken over the Old Testament as Scripture
would no doubt soon become acquainted with it.
But 'the red dragon' is more complex. Some
dragon imagery occurs in all ancient mythologies,
and appears in the Old Testament in the form of
'leviathan' or 'behemoth'. In Jewish apocryphal

literature the serpent of Eden becomes identified with the dragon as a symbol of evil power. It is probable that the colour and other details of the monster mentioned in Revelation 12 are mainly traditional.[12]

Behind the language used to describe the supreme agent of evil can be seen the conviction that evil forces, of a highly repugnant character, are at work on earth. The dramatic way in which the dragon sweeps a third of the stars to earth with its tail is intended to impress on the readers the strength of the opposition confronting them. The sheer ugliness of the imagery used emphasizes the unacceptable face of evil.

With a protagonist as evil and as powerful as this it is striking that two more beasts are needed to strengthen the imagery. The second and third beasts appear in chapter 13 after the dragon has gone off to make war with the woman and her offspring. The timing of the arrival of the other beasts is carefully planned. They are to be the dragon's agents. The first has a blasphemous name upon its heads, and it sustains a mortal wound which nevertheless heals. The parallel with the Lamb, once slain but now alive, is not far to seek. At this juncture, the trinity of evil must be introduced, for the aim of the second beast, which appears less overpowering than the first beast (it has only two horns instead of the first beast's ten horns), is to cause people to worship the beast who had sustained the mortal wound. The third component of the trinity of evil has precisely the same function as the Holy Spirit, in that he attempts to

---

12. For a thorough examination of the background of this dragon mythology cf. P. Prigent, *Apocalypse 12,* 120ff.

call forth worship not towards himself but towards another.

There is little profit in attempting to decipher the number 666. From earliest times a wide variety of suggestions were made, mainly based on the assumption that the enumeration must be made in Greek.[13] The almost unlimited number of suggestions must put us on our guard. The statement that the number is a human number (13:18) is perplexing in view of the fact that the beast is clearly a spiritual agency of evil. The implication is that this evil genius works through human agencies. Presumably the number 666 meant something to the original readers, but its enigmatic character should warn the modern reader not to assume too much. All that can safely be said is that the key is now lost. If of course the writer is implying that there is a definite connection between the reigning emperor and the dominant agent of evil, the use of the cypher could be explained by considerations of security.

We have yet to mention a particularly loathsome image which is used to describe the activity of the trilogy of beasts. Three foul frog-like spirits proceed from the mouth of the dragon and from the two beasts (16:13,14). The description of these foul spirits presents an impression of evil planning. In spite of their loathsome appearance they succeed in persuading the kings of the whole world to gather for the battle of Armageddon. That the kings could be seduced into this is a measure of their depravity. Here is a picture of human experience dominated by foul spiritual forces which shows how far the peoples of the earth have

---

13. Irenaeus, *Adv. Haer,* V. 29. 3ff, discusses several interpretations. He recognized that it was impossible to identify the number and treated it as symbolic of total apostasy.

strayed from the original purpose of the creator. If the picture is painted in lurid symbols this should not blind us to the poignant message it contains. We must enquire for the signs of such evil domination in our present world. The most optimistic among us cannot fail to see powerful forces at work in the affairs of men. The explanation that this is the result of the unleashing of diabolical forces may well be the only adequate one, in spite of the reluctance of many to recognize it.

We are introduced at the end of the book to a gorgeously dressed woman who has become intoxicated with the blood of the saints (17:1–6). She clearly represents the quintessence of opposition to God, here described not in terms of demonology, but in human terms. The fact that a woman is chosen must surely lead us to see her as a counterfeit of the Bride of the Lamb, who is not introduced until chapter 19. The woman is described as a harlot, in language which recalls an Old Testament description of those who were unfaithful to God.[14] She is full of blasphemous names and holds in her hand a cup full of abominations. A greater contrast with the Bride arrayed in fine pure linen could hardly be imagined. The purpose is to show what paradoxes evil agencies produce in human affairs. Externally 'Babylon' is splendid, but inwardly she is rotten to the core. It seems best to regard the harlot as symbolic of mankind opposed to God, just as the Bride stands for mankind redeemed by God and committed to his mission.[15] There is

---

14. Caird, *Revelation*, 212, draws attention to parallels with the mother goddess of Canaanite mythology which permeated Israelite religion. He connects the woman image of Babylon with the mention of Jezebel in 2:20.

15. As Beasley-Murray, *Revelation*, 250, points out, John is determined to present the woman in the strongest possible contrast to the Bride.

some significance in the harlot bearing the name of an important ancient city since the Bride comes to be identified as the New Jerusalem. The worst the dragon can do is to conjure up a pale imitation of God's plan but lacking all moral strength and doomed to destruction. The lament over the fall of Babylon in chapter 18 gathers within itself the lament of mankind through the ages, and not least in our day, over the sheer materialism and immorality of civilization. Its relevance needs no underscoring.

Our final comment on the symbols of evil concerns Death and Hades. These are symbols of man's last enemy. As early as ch. 1 the reader is assured that Christ has the keys to Death and Hades (1:18). They appear again on the opening of the fourth seal (6:8) where their mission is one of destruction. But Death and Hades at length meet their fate when they are cast into the lake of fire (20:14). Death is seen to have no place in God's redemptive plan and is ultimately banished. But the presence of this stalking personification through the pages of the book is a powerful reminder of the ravages effected by death through human history. Yet it meets its match in the final triumph of God.

The Background of Conflict

Conflict is a universal phenomenon. It arises from a variety of causes, but where it concerns super-natural forces some investigation of the background out of which it may have arisen is necessary as a prelude to understanding its significance. We shall consider various possibilites.

Greek dualism
It might be thought that this book is dualistic in

the Greek sense of the word, but this would be an inaccurate assessment.[16] At no point does evil have the complete mastery. Such freedom as it has to attack the people of God has been conferred upon it, and then only for a restricted period. The fundamental notion of this book is that God is sovereign and what he plans will ultimately happen. The ravages of evil are powerfully presented, but the amount of space devoted to the advances of evil is limited compared with that allocated to describing God's care for his people. The movement of the book, although it includes some scenes in which the church appears to be under very considerable stress, is inexorably directed toward the ultimate triumph of the Lamb.

The Old Testament
We must look elsewhere for the basic background for the conflict situation in this book. It is natural in view of the widespread use of Old Testament imagery to examine the Old Testament to discover whether it contains any suggestion of a combat situation which would provide a key to the understanding of this book. It must be admitted that as far as the history of Israel is concerned the Old Testament does not provide much evidence of a struggle between the forces of darkness and the forces of light. There is a hint of it in Isa. 27:1, but it is not prominent. What tension does exist is derived from the disobedience and failure of God's people. The record centres on the faithfulness of God to his covenant rather than on the adverse

16. The most notable of the commentators who appealed to pagan sources was W. Bousset, *Die Offenbarung Johannis*, Göttingen 1896. But he stressed Egyptian and Iranian mythology as parallels rather than Greek dualism. See also F. Boll, *Aus der Weltbild der Apokalypse*, Leipzig-Berlin 1914.

spiritual activities of the forces of darkness. In Job
we find Satan opposing a man of God, but he is not
yet portrayed in such 'diabolical' terms as in this
book. Nevertheless the serpent in Eden prepares
us to some extent for the clash of spiritual forces
on which later revelation focused.

Apocalyptic
It was during the age of the apocalyptists that
belief in the widespread activities of spiritual
forces developed to a significant extent. Not only
did this include belief in angels as agents entrusted
to carry out the will of God, a concept which could
find support from many passages in the Old
Testament, but it also included the idea of a
supreme ruler. Angelic activity affected many
aspects of life. Angels were believed to control the
seasons and they were responsible for the harvest.
They were also portrayed as maintaining the
heavenly records. There was a hierarchy of both
good and evil angels. During this period it was
increasingly supposed that the world was under the
influence of evil powers and that the great world
powers were consequently agencies of Satan.[17]
It was not difficult to perceive a person like Anti-
ochus Epiphanes as being an agent of the devil
against the people of God. There is no doubt that
such current ideas exerted a powerful influence on
the author of this book.

Like the author of the book of Revelation, the
apocalyptists rejected the Greek idea of two nearly
equal forces dominating the world. They believed

17. See Beckwith, *Apocalypse*, 70–71. Cf. also C. Rowland, *The
Open Heaven; Apocalypticism in the Mediterranean World* (ed.
D. Hellholm), Tübingen 1983; and *L'Apocalypse johannique* (ed.
J. Lambrecht), Leuven 1980.

the coming Messiah would overcome, not by military might, but by the breath of his mouth (2 Esd. 13:9ff; En. 62:2; PsSol 17:24; cf. 2 Thess. 2:8). In this there is remarkable agreement between their work and this book. We may also note a shared belief in the fate of the fallen angels in a fiery pit (En. 10:6;13; 90:25), and of Satan himself (Test. Jud. 25; Test. Levi. 18; Sib. Or. III 73; Ass. Mos. 10). In respect of the combat between good and evil it may be said that this book stands within the tradition of the Jewish apocalyptists.

Qumran
One of the characteristic features of the Qumran community was that its members believed themselves to have been placed within a conflict situation. The War document shows how fundamental the war imagery was to their very existence. But the coming conflict was not regarded by them as a spiritual battle so much as an actual war situation in which the Messiah would appear on their side.

Other New Testament Books
The Synoptic gospels contain many instances of exorcisms of evil spirits. These cases reflect a widespread belief in spiritual forces, often of an adverse kind, operating in human lives. They also show the power of Jesus to control them. Although in modern times the demonic element is played down, it is impossible to excise these cases from the gospels. The life of Jesus is presented in terms of his conflict with the forces of darkness. Two features are worth noting. The demons were rebuked and silenced when they bore testimony to Jesus, for he would not accept testimony from such a source. The gulf between the evil spirits

and Jesus could not be wider. The other evidence is the 'Beelzebub' issue in which his enemies charged Jesus with casting out demons through the prince of the demons. The absurdity of this charge is vividly brought out by the remark that Satan would not be divided against himself. The conflict situation is taken for granted.

In the Fourth gospel, the driving out of the prince of this world (12:31), which occurs in the passion of Jesus, focuses attention again on the conflict theme (see also 16:11). Here God confronts the prince of this world. Before Jesus is betrayed Satan entered into Judas Iscariot (13:27), and it is assumed without explanation that evil forces were arraying themselves against Jesus at the time of his passion. The conflict theme is also seen in John's gospel in the use of 'world' in a sense antagonistic to God (N.B. especially 15:18,19; 16:20; 17:14). The antipathy between God's people and the world aligns itself with the main antitheses in this book, between e.g. light and darkness, truth and error. Similar antitheses are found in the Qumran literature.

The same conflict theme is found in Acts, although here it is not so strongly expresed. There are still exorcisms, as for instance when Paul encounters the fortune-telling slave-girl and exorcizes the evil spirit. There is a sense in which happenings within the church may also be seen as due to Satanic activity, as in the case of Ananias and Sapphira (Acts 5:3). But the book is an account of the clash between Judaism and Christianity rather than a record of warfare between spiritual forces.

In his epistles Paul shows himself acutely conscious of the conflict. He sees the god of this world blinding the minds of unbelievers lest they should see the light of the gospel (2 Cor. 4:4).[18] There are spiritual antagonists who aim to defeat the spread of the gospel. Paul sees the Christian life in terms of warfare, in opposition to an enemy flinging flaming darts (Eph. 6:16). He even speaks in terms of spiritual forces of evil active in the heavenly places. He is aware in his own experience of opposition from the evil one (N.B. the messenger of Satan in 2 Cor. 12:7). He is convinced that neither angels nor demons can separate him from the love of Christ (Rom. 8:39). He can explain conversion in terms of deliverance from the kingdom of darkness and of transfer into the kingdom of the Son of God (Col. 1:13).

Paul's allusion to the return of Christ and his action against those who do not obey the gospel (2 Thess. 2:7–10) is strongly reminiscent of the theme of the book of Revelation.[19] In the same epistle the lawless one whose activity will precede the parousia acts in accordance with the work of Satan. The conflict theme here is strong. In 1 Timothy whatever is outside the church is seen as the sphere of Satan (1:20), while the times to come will be characterised by doctrines of demons, which are the antithesis of what God has designed. Enough has been said to demonstrate that Paul taught the same kind of spiritual combat as is found in the book of Revelation.

In conclusion, we note that the theme of spiritual conflict is present also in Heb. 2:14; Jas. 4:7; 1 Pet. 5:8; here is further evidence for the

---

18. The term 'god' is applied to Satan here because his followers treat him as such. Cf. P. E. Hughes, *Paul's Second Epistle to the Corinthians,* Grand Rapids 1962, 126, who notes that all false deities are regarded as no-gods.

19. Cf. I. H. Marshall's discussion in *1 and 2 Thessalonians,* London 1983, 196ff.

widespread influence of this idea. The Johannine
epistles are unique among New Testament books
in mentioning antichrist, not so much as the
supreme personification of evil, but rather as a
description of that class of people who deny Christ
(1 Jn. 2:22; 4:3; 2 Jn. 7).

We need not look far to find a striking modern
relevance in the conflict theme. It is not customary
to speak of the tensions and struggles of the
modern world in terms of a conflict of spiritual
forces. But our understanding would be clearer if
we could regain an insight into the background of
spiritual warfare; if we could detect the malicious
antagonism of Satanic forces; and if the spiritual
solution to the world's ills were more clearly seen
to rest in the victory of the Lamb.

Judgment

Twentieth century Christianity has seen a marked
movement away from the biblical theme of final
judgment. Realized eschatology attempts to get
away from judgment by viewing it as related to
historical action in the present.[20] In addition, it is
considered by many to be an alien concept in view
of the love of God. Resulting from this tendency
there is also an inadequate idea of righteousness.
Without some notion of judgment morality tends
to fail. Yet even those who deny to God any right
to act in judgment would be the first to protest if a
human judge dealt too leniently with a public
scandal. The fact is that in any ordered society

20. Cf. C. H. Dodd's view in *The Epistle of Paul to the Romans*,
London 1932, on 1:18 and 2:5ff. Cf. the discussion and critique of
Dodd's position by N. Q. Hamilton, *The Holy Spirit and Escha-
tology in Paul*, Edinburgh 1957, 66–67.

sanctions must be imposed on those who flout the regulations. Judgment cannot be dispensed with.[21] Certainly the most cursory reading of Revelation will demonstrate its importance within the book. Yet first impressions may mislead, for judgment is not the major theme. It is subsidiary to the theme of God's control of history and the assurance of his ultimate triumph.

The triple series of seven judgments in the seals, trumpets and bowls form part of the framework of the book. It is a matter of dispute whether these series are to be regarded as consecutive or concyclic, but there can be no doubt that they stress the inevitability of retribution on those who do not repent before God. It can scarcely be denied that there is some progression in the severity of the judgments. The intensity of the calamities reaches a climax in the pouring out of the bowls. But the most significant feature of these series is that in spite of their terrible nature men did not repent, but rather cursed God (cf. 16:9, 11). This would imply that the judgments are motivated not by vindictiveness, which would be alien to the concept of God seen in this book, but by mercy.

It must be admitted that the language used is vivid and at times horrific. The poet paints in startling colours, using bold strokes to express his conviction that God can do no other than judge evil. The book moves inexorably towards the great

21. J. Ellul, *Apocalypse*, New York 1977, 172, discusses various reasons for the dismissal of the judgment idea on the grounds that it is derived from outmoded ideas of spiritual conflicts or has developed from complexes or is an invention of those who exploit the poor. But scriptural teaching throughout supports the idea of a God who, because he is perfect and just, must be in conflict with a world which is not. For a detailed discussion of judgment, cf. L. Morris, *The Biblical Doctrine of Judgment*, London 1960.

white throne where final judgment is executed on all men. This does not appear out of place in the overall movement of ideas within the book. The throne of God has been in the background throughout the book and is central to the New Jerusalem. The thought moves naturally from one to the other. History cannot be consummated without some reckoning being made. In short, the philosophy of history is a moral one. Some scholars have made much of the motive of revenge in this book,[22] but although it is present it is not the most significant theme. The martyrs under the altar cry for vengeance (6:10), but there is no immediate response to that cry. They are merely given a white robe. At the conclusion of the dirge over fallen Babylon, the saints are called on to rejoice over her fall, but this is not expressed in terms of revenge.

An important aspect of the conflict theme in this book is the sharp division which is made between one side and the other. The antithesis between God and Satan is extended in other directions. The angelic agents of God are contrasted with the satanic retinue. The church of Christ is set over against the human dupes who carry out the satanic devices, especially the kings and rulers of the earth and those under their sway. The sharpness of the division is made more vivid by a twofold sealing operation. The servants of God are sealed (7:3) to set them apart, and these form the

---

22. Cf. A. Yarbro Collins, 'The Political Perspective of the Revelation of John', *JBL* 96, 1977, 241–256; W. Klassen, 'Vengeance in the Apocalypse of John', *CBQ* 28, 1966, 300–311. On Revelation 18, see Yarbro Collins's article in *L'Apocalypse johannique* (ed. Lambrecht) 185–204, and her article 'Persecution and Vengeance in the Book of Revelation' in *Apocalypticism in the Mediterranean World and the Near East* (ed. D. Hellholm) 729–750.

redeemed community. The rest are sealed with the mark of the beast (13:16). There is no middle way. The antithesis is total. This is also seen in the emphatic list of exclusions from the New Jerusalem (21:8).

We cannot escape from the message of this book regarding judgment. Its uncompromising stance serves as a challenge. There is no way of watering down the view of the consummation of history which it presents. In modern times when the theme of judgment is not to the fore in Christian teaching, this book serves as a timely reminder of the importance of aligning ourselves on the right side in the cosmic conflict.

Consummation

This is the only book in the New Testament which is detailed and specific concerning the winding up of the present age, although hints may be found elsewhere. This fact is clearly of immense importance in determining the relevance of the Christian faith for the present. No concept is satisfactory which excludes the future. There must be some notion about the winding up of history. The suggestion that the Christian faith can turn the present world into a coming Utopia which will continue for ever is not supported by this book. In fact the approach of Revelation to the present order is essentially pessimistic. All it is fit for is to pass away. Heaven and earth must give way to a new heaven and earth. The existing Jerusalem must give way to a New Jerusalem. Everything must become new (21:5). Such an uncompromising message sounds a death knell for a purely social gospel, although to recognise this is not to deny the social importance of the gospel in the present age.

The replacement of the existing order with one which is new and superior cannot be accomplished without a resolution of the present combat situation. This book with its strange poetic language shows the powerful forces of evil ultimately brought to nothing. There is never any doubt about the outcome. The Lamb is in control throughout. The displays of fury by antichristian forces are restricted in time and extent. The supreme message in this book is one of hope and encouragement. Let the devil do his worst—he cannot thwart the purposes of God. There is finally no future for him except the lake of fire.

What is most surprising is the means used to destroy those who oppose the Lamb. The final clash is expressed in military terms. The Victor rides a white horse and makes war (19:11), but there is no real battle. He brings with him the armies of heaven, who are dressed not in armour or military gear, but in wedding garments. The nations simply collapse under the devastating sword of the warrior-king, a weapon which is nothing other than his commanding word. The final denouncement of evil is majestically related. Its personification in the dragon and in the gaudily attired harlot, Babylon, contrasts vividly with the description of the bride and of the new Jerusalem. The book leaves the reader with the impression that however powerful the forces of evil appear to be, the reality is very different. Even the dragon can be subdued by a single angel with a single chain, apparently without a struggle.

The last two chapters offer a serene picture of a new type of community existence which comes as some relief after the fierce conflicts in the earlier part of the book. The New Jerusalem is clearly intended to contrast with the old, and yet it goes considerably beyond it in its scope. It is no longer restricted to Jewish concepts. It has no need of a temple, for God himself dwells there.[23] It stands for a universal community devoted to the worship of God. We have already seen that this is the perfect representation of the church. But why is it expressed in terms of a city? This is surprising in view of the fact that mankind began, according to Genesis, in a garden. Cities were made by man. Yet by virtue of this very fact cities represent humankind in community. The supreme example of humanity in community must be the church of Christ purified from all her blemishes.

The New Jerusalem descends from heaven after a new heaven and earth have been formed (21:1ff). Paradoxically no mention is made of the city descending to earth. Such a detail is clearly unimportant for the writer. What is crucial is the condition of existence in this idyllic place. God will be dwelling there and all pain will be banished. The details are intended to show God's perfect provision at the consummation of history. The beauties of the city are described in poetic language. Its gold and precious stones and its measurements and shape are symbolic. Its perfect cube is like the Holy of Holies, although of massive proportions. Its glory is God himself and the Lamb. Faced with this astonishing vision we may well ask what relevance it has for us to-day.

In answer to that question we may point to our pressing need for some concept of man living in perfect harmony and in ideal surroundings. We

---

23. E. Lohse, *Die Offenbarung des Johannes*, Göttingen 1960, 101, notes the indebtedness of Revelation 21 to Ezekiel 40–48, but points out the essential difference regarding the Temple in that vision and this.

need some assurance that redeemed humanity is of such a character that not only is harmonious social existence possible, but that men and women are actually destined for it in the purpose of God. This admittedly presents a different approach from much modern theology, especially that of liberation theology which aims to create a New Jerusalem in our present age through violent means. This book affirms that evil can be overcome only by spiritual means and once this is accomplished there is no bar to the establishment of a perfect society.

Conclusion

The twin themes of conflict and consummation are intended to be an encouragement to the Christian church. Those experiencing the conflict are assured of the victorious outcome. Whatever the weight of evil opposition, there is no possibility of its ultimate success. Persecution and tribulation have been the lot of God's people in all ages and this book has many times been a strong support to those who have suffered. The end of history is not spelled out in detail, but the final defeat of all oppressive forces is described in terse language. The fall of Babylon is symbolic of the collapse of all evil systems and civilizations and conveys strong consolation to those who are at present imprisoned within a seemingly impregnable system. The assurance that the consummation of history is not fortuitous, but is firmly in the hands of God, is of the highest relevance in an age threatened with nuclear self-destruction.

The New Jerusalem vision with which the book fittingly ends is a positive hope for all who have embraced the Christian gospel. The end of the present age will not come until the way has been opened for a glorious future which evil will be powerless to spoil.